Daniel Zangger Borch's

ULTIMATE
VOCAL VOYAGE

The definitive method for unleashing the rock,
pop or soul singer within you

D1613977

INNEHÅLL

Notfabriken

All excersises are written by Daniel Zangger Borch if nothing else is indicated.

Copyright © 2005 Notfabriken Music Publishing AB
Author: Daniel Zangger Borch
Translation: Craig Pratt
Illustrations: Katarina Lernmark
Cover & graphic prod: Elizabeth Friman & Leila Holmgren
Printed in: Mediagallerian, Bromma, Sweden 2007
Edition: 1:1
ISBN: 978-91-85575-19-0

Notfabriken

Daniel Zangger Borch was born and raised in Copenhagen, Denmark but has spent his adult life in Stockholm, Sweden. A professional singer for many years, Daniel has contributed his vocal talents to numerous CDs from hard rock band *Alien* to two Swedish Song Contests in the duo *Crosstalk* and has 2007 released a soul album of his own material.

Daniel is the first Swedish singing voice specialist to scientifically study the functioning of the rock, pop and soul voice. Drawing on his vast experience as a singer and educator and working in close collaboration with eminent vocal scientists, he has succeeded in developing a deceptively simple series of exercises that are guaranteed to help you reach your vocal potential. Although he may have one foot in the scientific community, the other remains firmly planted in the reality of life as a professional rock, pop and soul singer. The Zangger Borch method is designed to work in the real world.

Daniel is regularly hired as a guest speaker by teachers and singers all over Europe and also frequently works with top Swedish performers both as a vocal coach and producer.

Daniel has been in charge of vocal teaching at a number of teaching institutions such as the Stockholm Conservatory of Music, and regularly visits European music schools to share his methods. In 2003 Daniel started his own company *Voice Centre*, Stockholm, where he coaches, researches and produces.

5

Foreword

It is often said that the eyes are the windows of the soul! One could just as easily say that the voice is the window of your feelings! Every expression and emotional state is coloured or reflected by the voice; the loud, angry voice; the soft gurgling voice we use when we pout and talk "baby talk"; the chirping voice of lovers and the shaky nervous voice. Apparently it takes from one and a half to four minutes to form an impression of another person. Body language accounts for around half of the information we use as the basis for that impression and vocal characteristics for up to thirty eight percent. In other words, it's not what you say but rather how your body and voice reflect your choice of words. Obviously our voice plays a large part in the social theatre.

After two decades as a professional rock, pop and soul singer interspersed with teaching and research, I never cease to be amazed by how little we know about the intricate details of the voice. As yet there is still no instrument that can accurately measure the changes we feel in voices so we are forced to rely on our own perception. It is not uncommon that a singer may be hoarse and feel that their voice is not working properly even though a thorough examination may reveal no physical evidence of a problem. This is part of the enchantment of working with the voice. I would like to point out that even though I have attempted to base my methods on research results, my experience as a teacher and singer forms the basis of my teaching method.

The inspiration for this book came to me while I was recording the instructional video *Vocalist* (Bokmalen 1994). It took a bit over ten years, but I am just as passionate now as I was then about informing singers and those who work with them about the functions and possibilities of the voice. Whenever I meet students, performers, teachers and researches or visit institutions, I am struck by the emotions that the subject of singing arouses. When discussions arise as to what a particular register should be called or how a warm up should be performed tempers can flare and the intensity in the room can rival that of the floor of the New York Stock Exchange!

The music industry makes heavy demands of singers. Ideally the voice should be tireless! Long concert tours with constant interviews and promotional work, accessibility around the clock for morning TV programs or late night club gigs all take their toll. Singers often combine singing with other part-time jobs like waiting tables or leading play-groups, often in environments where dry air makes life for the vocalist even more difficult. Professions that work closely with singers often have little or no understanding of the limitation of the voice. Arrangers, production companies, record labels and musical directors alike should take it upon themselves to learn more about voice function. Understanding the singer who has been forced to say "no" because the hoarseness or pain of a cold has their voice on the defensive, should be a given.

Body and soul are closely intertwined. When the soul is healthy the body is free of tension and vice versa. It is therefore essential that we devote time and energy to maintaining the balance between body and soul. Stress adversely affects our general wellbeing and even impacts on the voice. In order to be able to use your voice effectively you will need to counteract the negative effects of stress. Relaxation and body awareness in conjunction with mental training increases the likelihood of being able to perform at the top of your daily form on every occasion. The voice is a complicated instrument and when it comes to technique and voice qualities there are many theories about what is right or wrong, often depending on the individual teacher's or listener's own musical experience, interest and taste.

Our reasons for singing are varied. One person may use it as safety valve to alleviate the pressures of a stressful life, another may be determined to become a star and a third may sporadically use it to add a little joy to their world.

To create a little perspective on how the voice works it is helpful to compare it to the rest of the body. The muscles, joints, ligaments and nervous system all react to activity. Stimulating a muscle makes it stronger whereas overexertion will wear it out. If a nervous system impulse is impaired you will work at half speed resulting in uneven loading which leads to wear and pain. What I'm trying to say is that if you want to be a full-time singer you will need to develop your technique, strengthen your muscles and ligaments and your reflexes in the same way as a professional athlete. This requires daily training. If you want to use your voice more sporadically the effort required would correspond to that of the average person who exercises to stay in shape. i.e. one or two sessions a week.

Continuing with the athletics analogy, if you run 10 km you cannot expect to run at the same pace you would for a 100 m sprint. Likewise, if you sing a whole evening you cannot be expected to sing at the top of your range for the duration of the performance. If you don't warm up you may pull a muscle, if you don't stretch you may swell and stiffen up. Just as with runners, there are sprinters and long distance types. I'm not saying that one is better than the other but it is certainly something you should be aware of when making demands on your voice. This will make it easier to grasp the reasoning presented here about warming up, cooling down, voice care etc.

Technique should be practised when rehearsing. By the time you perform your technique should have been consolidated to the point where you are free to concentrate on expression. Ultimately, the purpose of working hard on your technique is to give you the ability to express yourself as freely and as often as you like.

Many thanks to ...

My partner Sara for being my eternal sounding board, for your patience and inspiration and for lending your vocal talents to the accompanying CD.

To my children Jessica, Alex and Elton because you're wonderful.

To my father MD Professor Kurt Borch for putting up with my trying telephone calls on medical matters.

Retired Professor of Music Acoustics Johan Sundberg, my main source of inspiration, for your knowledge and the natural way you have shared it with me. Thank you for your patience and proof reading of both the Swedish and English versions of this book.

Gunlis Österberg for your positive attitude and ability to edit and interpret my sprawling texts.

Margareta Thalén for meaningful feedback in the early stages of this project.

Arne Tengstrand for playing the digital piano on the CD.

Per-Åke Lindestad MD, Ph.D for many years of good advice and for your pointers to the chapter *Voice Care and Voice Disorders*

Stellan Hertegård MD, Ph.D for going over the chapter *This is your Voice.*

Staffan Wilén MD, for your interesting angles on the chapter *Voice Care and Voice Disorders.*

Mats Granberg for your technical consultation.

Rolf Christersson for letting me use your sayings in the book.

The Patricia Grammings Memorial Trust for financial support for my research projects.

SMI (Stockholm Institute of Music Educators) for financial support through artistic development.

Jan Löw for the musical transcriptions

Craig Pratt for his translation and creative input.

Ingemar Hahne and all the other stalwarts at Notfabriken for believing in me and making the project a reality.

9

Notfabriken

I:Introduction

If you come across something you don't understand, refer to the comprehensive glossary at the end of the book. There you'll find specific terms and slang expressions for a lot of the things that are unique to the vocal and music business. In order to understand the exercises it is also important that you are familiar with the chapter Pronunciation and symbols. The symbols presented there are taken from the Standard American Vowel Key.

On the accompanying CD it's "ladies first" as the exercises are sung first by a female voice. After that the guys get their turn to practice when the exercise is sung by a male voice. The recordings are not necessarily in the same key as the corresponding notation but will nevertheless give you a clear idea of how the exercises are to be performed. There are also more variations of certain exercises in the book than on the CD. A book can never replace a good teacher but it can be a useful complement to your lessons. If you would like more information on Zangger-Borch's Ultimate Vocal Voyage contact Voice Centre Stockholm or go to **www.voicecentre.se** which is continually being updated.

In order to get an overview of the elements that contribute to the development of your voice it can be useful to divide them up into a "voice pie".

The pie can be divided into the three "T's"

– Taking care of
– Technique
– inTerpretation

All voice training involves at least one of these "slices". You can even turn the whole thing around: To be able to freely interpret you need good technique and to improve your technique you need to take care of your voice. Train the different elements side by side.

You can't train technique for an extended period without including interpretation and it would not serve you to just interpret songs and neglect your technique. You can neither interpret nor train your technique if you fail to take care of your voice so that it is in the best possible shape both when you practice and perform.

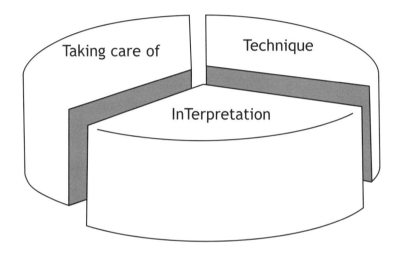

Notfabriken

PRONUNCIATION & SYMBOLS

To get the desired results out of the exercises it is important that your pronunciation is correct which is why I have included the table below. This book uses American English symbols. Using the pronunciation on the CD as a guide is fine, but if you don't have the CD at hand you should refer to the table.

This is by no means a complete phonetic overview and is intended as a tool to help you understand the exercises in the book. As such I have only used the vowels, diphthongs and consonants that appear in the book. The phonetic symbol for consonants is often the same alphabet's corresponding lower case letter so I have only given consonant sounds where they differ.

Vowels	REPRESENTATIVE WORDS	INTERPRETATIVE SPELLING	PHONETIC SYMBOL
	father	"AH"	[a:]
	run	"ah"	[a]
	kids	"ih"	[i:]
	fresh	"eh"	[e]
	she	"EE"	[i:]
	move	"OO"	[u:]
	clover	"oh"	[o:]
	bird	"UH"	[ɝ:]
Diphthongs	time	"ay"	[aɪ]
	toy	"oy"	[oɪ]
	how	"ow"	[au]
	hay	"ey"	[eɪ]
Consonants	B (*flapping lips*)	"B"	[B]
	song	"ng"	[ŋ]
	ship	"sh"	[ʃ]

Notfabriken

Fibre binds water in your stomach. If you eat a lot of whole grain foods you will therefore need to drink extra water.

Whoever reads this book, regardless of whether they are a singer or a teacher, is a student. Studying this subject, either to put it into practice yourself or to pass the contents on to someone else, requires that you are both open to new approaches are free from preconceived ideas. We are all life-long students in some form and this means that ultimately it is up to us to decide what is to be learnt, why and in which way. Good luck!

ON EDUCATION....

"The individual human himself is the only one that can be active in such a way as to facilitate learning. All a teacher can do is to create suitable external conditions for learning and to stimulate the individual's activity"
John Steinberg

Notfabriken

II: Warming up

Why should you warm up? Many singers have asked that question and there is one definitive answer; it is necessary to be able to use your voice optimally for prolonged periods. Unfortunately rock, pop and soul singers are often sceptical about the benefits of warming up, so to help make the point it is useful to compare singing to other types of physical activity. There probably aren't that many athletes who do not stretch and warm up prior to a competition. Even the man in the street has learnt the importance of a warm up before jogging or taking an aerobics class. Skipping it can lead to pulled or torn muscles and even painful joint and muscle conditions. Singers are voice athletes and should train and take care of their voice in the same way that athletes take care of their bodies. We often take our voices for granted; they're expected to work on demand and ideally be in top shape whenever they are called upon! But singing is no different from any other physical activity and failing to warm up will impair your ability to perform and may even result in injury. In short: warm up your body and voice for optimal performance and to prevent injury.

This chapter presents an exercise routine to help you take care of your voice by warming it up before a performance. Each exercise is fundamental for preventing unnecessary wear and to minimize possible swelling and overexertion. Warming up and preparing for a performance also includes finding your own strategy and rituals to ensure you can give your utmost when it really counts. Preparation may consist of testing your daily form in various ways; eating fruit, throat lozenges or chewing gum; perhaps drinking hot water and honey or going over lyrics and between song patter. Some singers prefer to be alone before going onstage whilst others are energised by being around their fellow musicians.

POSTURE

Good posture improves your ability to control your breathing and is the basis of good vocal technique. Controlled breathing reduces the strain on your vocal folds. By the time we are adults our posture has often deteriorated and the back and stomach muscles that are vital for vocal functioning have become weaker.

The muscles that we use to control our breathing demand that the body is balanced from top to toe. The front of our ankles and our pelvis are the foundation of our balance system. The rest of the body is stacked on top of these points. Generally speaking the body should be balanced over the front of our ankles when we stand and in line with our pelvis when we sit.

Here is a run through of the elements that contribute to good posture.

Exercise no.1 - Standing posture

A/ Feet

– Stand with your feet a hip's breadth apart.
– Stand on your toes.
– Lower yourself slowly until your heels just touch the floor.
– Remain in this position.

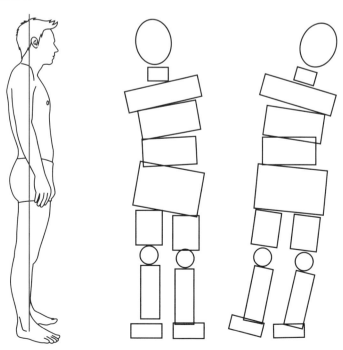

Now you should be nicely balanced! Repeat this a few times until you can identify that feeling of good balance. Putting too much weight on your heels can increase the strain on your larynx for example.

A suitably relaxed and balanced position may feel like you are leaning slightly forward with your weight on the front of your ankles.

B/ Knees

– Make sure your knees are not locked out as they often are when we rest our muscles.

C/ Hips

– Arch your back.
– Hunch your back.
– Position your pelvis in between these two extremes.
– Now your hips and pelvic floor should be straight.

The hips are connected to the large muscle groups. Joints and ligaments in our backsides, torso, legs and back work with the lower section of our breathing musculature. It is therefore important not to hunch or arch your back.

D/ Chest, Upper back and Shoulders

– Point your diaphragm straight ahead and focus your awareness by expanding your ribcage. (Once again make sure that you don't arch your back).
– Let your arms feel long.
– That's it! Now your shoulders will have naturally fallen into place.

If you sit a lot during the day your muscles will have weakened so it will be natural for your chest to sink and your shoulders to move forward. It is therefore very important to have strong back muscles and to stretch out your chest muscles. This posture can be tiring for the back muscles at first but light resistance training, stretching and good posture will soon increase your strength.

E/ Neck and Head

– Make your neck as long as possible without looking down.
– Do not clench your jaw.
– Your neck should now be in an ideal position.

It is difficult to give instructions about the head as we move it constantly when we interact with other people and situations. A lot of sitting in front of the computer can for example lead to the habit of jutting your chin out. This can cause tension in your neck which in turn can lead to headaches, dizziness and voice problems.

Now your posture should be excellent which is essential for controlling your breathing. It may feel a little stiff until your muscles get used to it. It is also important to maintain good posture when we move as we usually move when we sing.

Exercise No. 2 - Sitting posture

Singing sitting down is common when you work as a bar pianist or perform "unplugged" with a band. The strength of the muscles that regulate lung pressure is more accessible when you're standing up. This means that it is easier to sing *loudly* when standing, although it may be possible to sing *longer* when sitting. Good posture can help to even out these differences. When sitting, it is important to have a secure foothold and to maintain good posture from the hips up.

A/ Feet & knees

– Place your feet firmly on the floor.
– Sit out towards the edge of the chair.
– Make sure you are balanced.

It often feels better to place one foot directly under your upper body.

B/ Hips

– Make sure your hips/pelvis are straight (don't arch or bend your back).

C/ Chest/Upper back & Shoulders

– Straighten you spine (don't hunch or arch your back).
– Place your hands on your knees (if you're not holding a microphone of course).
– Let your upper arms "feel" long
– That's the way! Now your shoulders will naturally fall into a comfortable position.

D/ Neck & head

– Concentrate on the feeling of having a long neck.
– Do not clench your jaw.

 Your head and neck should now be in a good position

WARMING UP YOUR BODY

Warming up before singing increases the blood flow through your entire body, including those parts involved in the production of your voice. As many singers can testify, even moderate voice activity requires a lot of energy. Think about the pathetic, creaky tone of our voice when we are tired and lethargic. We clearly need a large portion of bodily presence, power and energy to prepare the voice to perform. Warming up your body means:

Notfabriken

- Increasing activity in the body which enlarges the blood vessels allowing more oxygen to be transported to the muscles.
- The increased supply of oxygen and the flexing and relaxing of muscles increases the temperature in the muscle. We warm up, the muscles become more supple and the risk of injury is reduced.

Getting your breathing going helps to heat up your muscles. During the following exercises breathe in deeply through your nose and out through your mouth.

Exercise no. 3 - Stretching your body

A/ Neck

- Slowly tilt your head to the left, Breathe.
- Tilt your head to the right: Breathe.
- Lift your head back up to its normal position.
- Place your hands on your collarbones and pull downwards.
- Slowly tilt your head backwards while opening your mouth. Jut your bottom jaw out (as if you had an underbite) 3–5 times.
- Let your head fall slowly forward until your chin is almost resting on your chest, breathe.

B/ Shoulders

- Place each hand on its corresponding shoulder and twist your body from side to side while making alternate circles in the air with your elbows. Keep your hips fixed.
- Make large movements so that you stretch all the way down to your lower back.
- Repeat the movement 10 times.
- Breathe briskly.

C/ Back

- Interlock your fingers behind your back and push your chest out, breathe in.
- Push your hips forward and then stretch your back like a cat, breathe out.
- Repeat.

Notfabriken

D/ Ribcage

– Stretch your right arm up in the air.
– Bend it over your head and bend your torso to the left as you point your left hand at the floor to the right of you. Look at the upper hand. Breathe.
– Swap sides and repeat.

E/ General

– Squat down.
– Rock backwards and forwards a little while breathing in.
– Stand up on the tip of your toes and stretch upwards as far as you can. Breathe out.
– Shake your whole body loose.

You didn't forget to breathe deeply in through your nose and out through your mouth did you?

VOICE MASSAGE

Massage can affect the voice in many ways and clinical tests have shown that one's speaking voice can be lowered by as much as a whole tone, which naturally helps to reduce voice strain. But something that is even better for the voice is "Voice massage", a well-established method for reducing tension in the vocal muscles. Ideally it should be performed by a trained massage therapist, however there are certain techniques that we singers can include in our daily voice care routine. The idea is to relieve tension that builds up as a result of stress, bad habits, poor posture, repetitive movements or clenched jaws. Signs that you may be in need of professional voice massage are:

– A hoarse speaking voice even though you haven't over-exerted it.
– Neck pain.
– Headache.
– Dizziness.

It is a good idea to check these things daily as even one night of jaw clenching is enough to affect your voice.

Notfabriken

Your brain can only maintain maximum concentration when learning for approximately twenty minutes

Exercise no. 4 - Voice massage

In order to remain as relaxed as possible, make sure you calmly breathe in through your nose and out through your mouth when performing these exercises.

A/ Head

– The area under your scalp is where many of your facial and neck muscles are attached. This makes scalp massage particularly pleasant and relaxing.
– Place your fingertips in the middle of your scalp and massage.
– Move them around making sure to cover the entire area.

B/ Temples

– Place your thumbs on your temples and massage your hair line with your fingers.
– Hold your fingers still and massage your temples with your thumbs.

C/ Face

– Grimace, screwing your face up as hard as you can.
– Open your mouth as wide as you can.
– Pretend you've got no teeth.
– Pout.

D/ Jaw muscles

– Place one palm against your cheek.
– Clench your jaw and locate your jaw muscles on the other side of your face with the finger tips of your other hand.
– Relax your jaw and massage the biggest muscles for about twenty seconds.
– Clench your jaw again to once again locate the muscles.
– Press firmly into the muscle with your index and middle fingers for about twenty seconds until you feel that it begin to soften.
– Press your thumbs onto your cheek-

bones. Slide down maintaining the pressure until you locate the area that is most tender. Stop for a few seconds and then release.
– Repeat the whole process on the other side of your face.

E/ Tongue root and tongue body

– Starting at the inside end of your lower jaw bone, massage your tongue root, working your way out to your chin. Note that there are lymph glands located along your jawbone. These feel like small balls and should not be pressed.

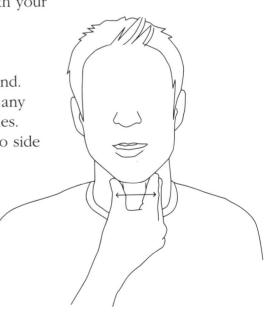

F/ Tongue

– Stick your tongue out and try to touch your chin. Keep extended for three seconds.
– Stick your tongue out and try to touch the tip of your nose. Keep extended for three seconds.
– Clean every surface of your teeth with your tongue.

G/ Larynx

– Gently hold your larynx with one hand.
– Open your mouth slightly to release any tension in your throat and jaw muscles.
– Gently move your larynx from side to side with rapid movements.

Many people experience discomfort when they touch the larynx due to the creaking that occurs as the thyroid and cricoid cartilages touch. This exercise should therefore be performed carefully. If it is performed correctly and you are sufficiently relaxed it is an effective tool for alleviating tense vocal folds and a fixed larynx.

H/ Throat

– Look down and to one side and grab the muscle that runs from your collar bone to behind your ear.
– Look straight ahead and massage it from the bottom up.
– Repeat on the other side.

Try to penetrate as deeply as possible into the muscle as this is where tension usually builds up.

Notfabriken

VOCAL WARM UP

The strain on your voice will vary from day to day depending on if you use it a lot (concert, rehearsals) or not at all. This makes it difficult to formulate hard and fast rules for vocal warm ups e.g. how long it should last and at how long it should be performed before singing. There are however, a few rules of thumb that can help guide you to the optimal warm up strategy. For example "short performance-long warm up, long performance-short warm up". It is also important not to sing louder or higher than you're voice is prepared for. Singing loudly is the last thing you want to do during a warm up.

I recommend that you warm up a fair while ahead of the performance and that you should be ready approximately 10 minutes before going on. This will allow your vocal folds and other laryngeal muscles to rest before the concert. Using the sports analogy again, most athletes warm up around an hour before a competition and use the remaining time for mental rehearsal.

We will start with a few exercises that, in my opinion, form a solid basis for a vocal warm up routine without wearing out your voice. The exercises consist of sounds that are produced by constricting the flow of air. When a constriction is created by the lips and tongue less load is placed on the vocal folds.

Exercise no. 5 – Morning callisthenics [w]

This is a good way to get your voice started, particularly in the mornings.

– Form your lips as if you were about to say "Why".
– Stop at "w" and don't pronounce the "ay".
– Imagine that you have a hot potato in your mouth.
– Glide from the bottom of your vocal range upwards as indicated in the diagram below.

To learn the exercise properly you can start by using a drinking straw. Eventually you can remove the straw and perform the exercise without it.

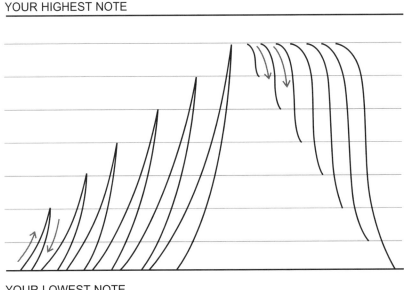

YOUR HIGHEST NOTE

YOUR LOWEST NOTE

This exercise is not enhanced by a melody. Rather, the most important aspect of this part of the warm up is to keep your larynx in as low a position as possible while working through your entire vocal range. The suggested duration of this exercise is three to five minutes. Why not treat it as a bit of light humming while you're in the shower or brewing the morning coffee?

Exercise no. 6 - Universal tool "B"

Jut your bottom jaw out to form an underbite, stick out your bottom lip and "*broom*" like a car. Until you have mastered the technique it may help to imagine your neck being as wide as an angry cobra and holding your fingers three centimetres over and to the side of the corners of your mouth.

A/

This exercise is performed glissando.

B/

This exercise is quite advanced and can be successively built upon by those of you who easily mastered example A. The melody is almost exactly the same as the previous one.

27

These exercises are not as easy as they sound and many people have difficulties when first attempting them. Don't give up - they are really worth the trouble. If you can't get your lips to vibrate, or if they stop vibrating, it is usually because of an imbalance between the pressure from your breathing muscles and the relaxation of your lips, cheeks and tongue. You could say that the slower your lips vibrate, the better your breathing and articulation will work together.

Exercise no. 7 – The Turtle dove [r]

CD 3

Roll an [r] to sound like a dove. This is a descending melody and is rhythmically quite difficult. It may help to put an [h], [k] or [d] before the [r] if you have difficulty getting your tongue rolling.

Just as in exercise no. 6 difficulty maintaining the vibration may be due to an imbalance between your breathing and articulation, but don't give up. If you can't make it work even after repeated attempts try replacing the [r] with [v].

CD 4

Exercise no. 8 – Asleep on the bus "ng"

28

Make the sound "ng" as in "song". Relax your jaw as if you had fallen asleep with your mouth open. Concentrate on the sensation of having clogged nasal cavities (just like when you have a cold). You may find that the higher up in your range you start the more you may need to open your mouth. Sing the high notes softly gradually increasing your volume as the exercise progresses. Be aware of possible tension in your jaw.

If you still don't feel sufficiently warmed up after performing these exercises you may add exercise no. 11 on page 36 (performed with crescendo/diminuendo) and exercises 18 and 19 on page 42 (add an "EE" or an "oh").

Vocal warm up – Things to remember

- If you sing every day it will take less time to get going. If you sing more sporadically it will take longer.
- Perform all exercises softly, but not so softly that you stop producing a tone. Be aware of tension.
- Feel free to divide the vocal warm up into two parts with several minutes rest in between.
- If you tire when warming up you are doing something wrong. Warning signs of vocal fatigue can include a dull ache in your throat, a dry, ticklish cough or your voice "breaking" easily.

It is natural for your voice to "rattle "a little as mucous begins to loosen up. But however tempting it may be, don't clear your throat. Drink some water instead and continue gently warming up. Your voice should clear fairly quickly.

VOCAL SOUND CHECK

This is not to be confused with warming up. In my opinion they are two different things and different methods should be used. We have already looked at warming up and why it is necessary for all singers. Not all singers need to fine tune their sound prior to performing. You may need to check your technique in certain parts of your range or assure yourself that the range and interpretative tools you need for the performance are accessible.

Professional singers who perform several times a week often need to warm up but seldom to fine tune their technique. If you work with your voice often enough you will be well aware of how to adjust your technique to produce the sound you require. It becomes a question of muscle memory and occurs in a split second.

The effects of physical training last for forty eight hours, so the ideal training interval should be every other day.

Some singers are happy enough ascending and descending through their range for a while with sounds like "oh "and "hey". Don't forget that a little movement and clapping can enhance the musicality and bring out the pleasure we find in singing, something that can only be of benefit prior to a performance.

Notfabriken

SUMMARY- WARMING UP

– Singers are voice athletes and should train and take care of their voices in the same way athletes take care of their bodies.

– Warming up your body, performing voice massage and a vocal warm up are essential for preventing unnecessary voice wear.

– The front of your ankles and your pelvis are the foundations of good balance.

– It is natural for your chest to sink in and your shoulders to slump forwards, especially if your muscles have become weaker due to prolonged periods of sitting. It is therefore vital to strengthen your back muscles and stretch your chest muscles.

– Voice massage is an established method for relieving tension in the muscles that are necessary for voice function. Tension can arise due to poor posture, repetitive movements or the unconscious jaw clenching associated with stress.

– A vocal sound check is used to find a sound or check the daily form of your voice.

Notfabriken

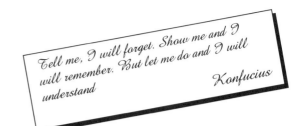

III: Breathing

Breathing is to a singer as petrol is to a car. It is absolutely essential to be in control of your breathing and in this chapter we will examine both the theory and practice you need to achieve this.

Breathing is one of the most important regulatory tools at a singer's disposal. Good breathing strategy will allow you to deliver air to your laryngeal muscles with finely tuned flow and pressure. It is also a prerequisite for long term vocal health and will help ensure years of singing pleasure no matter how you intend to use your voice or the style of music you sing.

Breathing is generally divided into two categories:

– Passive breathing
– Active breathing

Passive breathing uses approximately half a litre of air per breath and is repeated around twelve times per minute. The purpose of passive breathing is quite simply, to keep us alive. Active breathing is where you consciously regulate the pressure at which the air leaves your lungs and plan your inhalation and exhalation. When you sing you should be breathing actively. A description of a typical pattern of breathing while singing could be: Short inhalation - long exhalation.

INHALATION

Inhalation creates the conditions necessary for the larynx and the muscles associated with exhalation to be able to work optimally. You will now get to practice activ breathing through your nose and mouth.

Where inhalation is concerned you should remember two things:

Plan your breath

Many singers are in the habit of holding their breath between phrases and then hurriedly attempting to fill their lungs a few milliseconds before the next phrase starts. This rapid inhalation means that the air is cold and drying and you create tension in the vocal folds as they are kept closed.

Open your vocal folds as widely as possible

To prevent the vocal folds' mucous membranes (mucosa) from drying out from the hundreds of breaths taken during every performance it is important to open them as widely as possible when inhaling. This reduces their contact with the inhaled air. The feeling can be compared to the beginning of a yawn or being surprised.

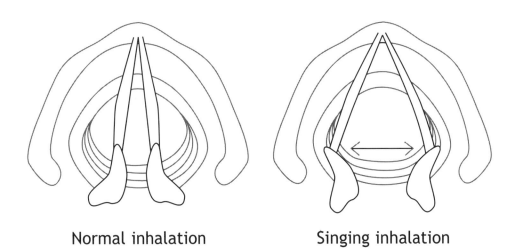

Normal inhalation   Singing inhalation

Notfabriken

Exercise no. 10 – Planning your inhalation through your mouth

Breathe through your mouth as shown in the notes below. Choose whatever note and vowel sound you like but make sure the notes are held for their full duration. Remember the feeling of yawning or being surprised while breathing in. Relax your breathing muscles as soon as the phrase ends and breathe passively until the next notated inhalation starts. Using a metronome will help you perform this exercise. (80 bpm).

After performing this exercise it may be appropriate to plan your breathing for several songs. Note the length of pauses and phrases and make notes to help you plan your breathing.

SUPPORT

Support! Sing from your stomach! Tummy out! Tummy in! Expand your ribcage! There are many expressions for the muscle activity that singers use to control lung pressure. But one word should have pride of place on the list: balance! A common misconception about support is that your abdominal, back and intercostal muscles should be rock hard and you should give it all you've got! However, it is actually more a question of control and, as is the case with all techniques, more effort is required when learning than when you have mastered it. In order for your breathing to provide support, air must be delivered to your larynx with exactly the right pressure for the required note. Muscles that work too hard hinder the process rather than help it and are not considered supportive. Likewise, tension may arise in the larynx if the activity of the breathing apparatus is too weak. Support is supposed to help and when you manage to control your breathing it can support your larynx. Something to consider when dealing with support is utilising some of the muscles used for inhalation even when exhaling.

There are many traps to avoid when it comes to breathing and support but the most common is probably pushing too hard when singing. If the air delivered to the larynx is under too much pressure the vocal folds will have to fight to hold back some of it while simultaneously producing a tone. This strains the voice. The correct strategy is to create exactly the correct lung pressure for the note you want to sing. A loud, high pitched note sung in the chest register requires more support than a softer note at a comfortable pitch.

Physical training that builds sufficiently strong muscles and increases your fitness can only help your breathing. Strong muscles help to maintain the good posture required for proper support, while increased fitness will improve your oxygen uptake. (You should however avoid training on the same day as an important performance)

It is important not to perform all of the breathing exercises one after the other. You may hyperventilate and feel dizzy.

Taking in large volumes of air as in the next exercise involves not only the abdominal and intercostals but also the muscles of the lower back. You should feel them working at the end of phrases when you start to run out of air.

Exercise no. 11 - Even flow "ih"

CD 6

- Stand with the entire length of your back against a wall.
- Place your feet a hip's breadth apart about 20 cm out from the wall.
- Note that a space forms in the curve of your lower back.
- Breathe in through your nose. When breathing out maintain an even airflow while making the sound "ih" for as long as possible. Increase the flow of air if the tone fluctuates.
- When you feel that you are almost out of air, close the space formed between your lower back and the wall by tilting your hips forward. This activates the broad spinal erector muscles and squeezes out any remaining air utilising your full lung capacity. This may well save you at the end of long phrases.

Train each vowel sound in any order you like.

Note different airflow required for each vowel and work on being able to sustain each vowel sound for about the same length of time. Perform this exercise in a comfortable key and for no more than five minutes at a time. When you are satisfied with the way you perform the exercise do it without the support of the wall.

Exercise no. 12 - Groovy "sh"

CD 7

Place your hands on your waist or on your diaphragm and cough! The muscle activity you feel is to be reproduced in time with the notes in the following exercise. Keep your shoulders still and let your breathing apparatus do the work.

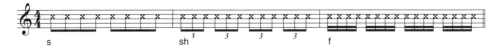

Notfabriken

Exercise no. 13 - Washboard "vah"

CD 8

This exercise is performed with a short voiced "v" prior to the vowel. Make sure you have time to relax your breathing muscles between each note.

Exercise no. 14 - Yielding "you don't know"

CD 9

The first part of this exercise is sung staccato which will mean that your breathing muscles will be working in an on/off way between every syllable. The second part is sung legato and with a crescendo. This means that your breathing muscles will work successively harder as the notes increase in volume.

BREATHING FOR RELAXATION

Stress can be anybody's Achilles heel, including singers. How our breathing affects the way we deal with stress is well documented and the number of relaxation exercises based on breathing is infinite. Of all the breathing techniques I have used to handle stress and clear my mind the following exercise is the one that has worked best. The combination of placing your fingers between your eyebrows and focusing on your breathing prevents you from being distracted by stressful thoughts.

Notfabriken

Your vocal folds vibrate 250 000 – 500 000 times per day depending on the pitch of your speaking voice.

Exercise no. 15 - Breathing to relax

- Place the index and middle fingers of your right hand between your eyebrows.
- Place your thumb and ring finger over your nostrils.
- Close one nostril with your thumb and breathe deeply and calmly through the other nostril.
- Release your thumb, close the other nostril with your ring finger and breathe deeply and calmly.
- Close your eyes and repeat the exercise slowly for three minutes.

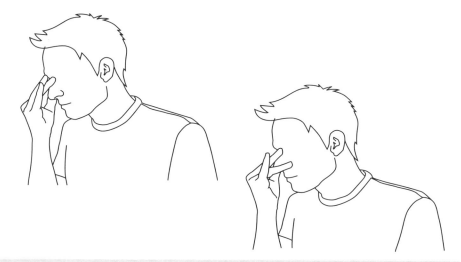

SUMMARY - BREATHING

- A typical breathing pattern while singing is short inhalation – long exhalation.

- A good breathing strategy is necessary for keeping your voice in top shape.

- Moderate physical training benefits your breathing and thereby your voice.

- Make sure you breathe in well before the start of a phrase and relax your breathing muscles as soon as a phrase ends.

- Breathing in through your nose warms the otherwise cold/cool air.

- Support means control of your breathing and the correct adduction for the required tone.

Notfabriken

IV: The vocal folds

The vibrations that are necessary to produce sound occur in the vocal folds (sometimes referred to as vocal cords). They also play the major roll in determining the register, pitch and volume of the tone produced and if it is breathy or pressed. The fundamental frequency of our voice is also governed by the vocal folds. Long, thick vocal folds result in a low fundamental frequency while short and thin produce a higher fundamental frequency.

Rock, soul and pop styles can trace their roots back to African American "call & response" and the English ballad tradition. This form of expression was originally an extension of talking - the vocals were simple and speech-like and the purpose was to tell stories, convey messages and feelings. Of course these styles have developed over time and the vocals have become more technical, but the origins were simple. It may help to remember this when you find yourself in the grip of performance anxiety struggling to find the most technically advanced vocal expression. It is therefore natural for those of us who sing in these genres to base our vocals on our speaking voice and then experiment with ways to develop our sound and phrasing.

In this chapter we will look at how to start and end a note, train in equalising and separating your registers and using a breathy, flowing or pressed tone. We will also be applying exercises for your chest and falsetto registers before progressing onto vibrato and vocal riffing.

RANGE

The term range refers to the area between the highest and lowest notes you can produce in a controlled manner. A vocal range of around two octaves is quite common and generally considered a prerequisite for working as a professional singer. However, just where these two octaves are located is less important as transposing songs to suit the singer is common practice in the rock, pop and soul genres.

Being able to use different nuances throughout your range is vital, as is mastery of both loud and soft tones in your chest and falsetto registers. Unfortunately there is a degree of "pitch hysteria" in the rock genre and singers are often forced to sing in high keys regardless of their gender or physical capabilities. This may be because a lot of energy is required to sing high and loud and this is seen to be in keeping with the high energy ethos of rock. I would like to stress that each singer should develop their range on the basis of their actual physical capabilities and then choose suitable material or transpose to a more comfortable key where necessary. We will now look at the factors that determine a singer's ability to broaden and utilise their entire vocal range.

– The length and thickness of their vocal folds
– The elasticity of their vocal folds
– The condition of the muscles that stretch their vocal folds

As mentioned previously, those with long, thick vocal folds will have a lower fundamental frequency than those with short and thin. The elasticity of the vocal folds also plays an important role in that the more elastic they are the easier it will be for the muscles to stretch them out to reach higher notes. Imagine two rubber bands. If you cut two rubber bands of the same size it is likely that you will be able to stretch one more than the other. This is due to the inherent elasticity of the material. Highly elastic material can stretch further than less elastic material. Vocal range is highly individual and you should aim to broaden *your* range on the basis of *your* physical characteristics and not compare yourself to other singers.

ONSETS AND OFFSETS

The fact that you start and finish a note several times per phrase and at least once after every breath makes this extremely important from a voice care perspective. A hard onset (start) occurs when the vocal folds close before the air stream starts and an abrupt offset (ending) occurs when your vocal folds come together forcefully (glottal stop) and then immediately release air (like a voiced sigh). Starting and ending notes in this way has become a popular embellishment.

A breathy onset occurs when the air stream start the vocal folds before they are brought together and a breathy offset occurs when the vocal folds are gradually deactivated. In other words you can start and end notes in several ways:

– Breathy
– Hard
– Simultaneous
– Creaky

Exercise no. 16 - Where the action is

– Hold your breath and open your mouth.
– Release small bursts of air.
– Can you hear or feel a clicking sound in your throat? This is your vocal folds closing with a little glottal stop!

In the following exercise we will try various types of onsets and offsets in order to be able to identify them and use them on demand, something that is useful both from an artistic and voice care perspective.

Exercise no. 17 - On off "get up"

CD
10

Here we will try the different approaches one after the other: Breathy-hard-simultaneous

Remember that there are as many ways to release a note as there are to start it: try starting or ending a note abruptly, breathily or creakily.

Notfabriken

CLOSING IN

When the vocal folds come together (adduct) and starts to vibrate, air passes through the glottis. The amount of air that passes through glottis depends on how hard you adduct your vocal folds and on your lung pressure, this also determines the quality of the note, from breathy, when adduction is faint and lung pressure is low, to pressed when adduction is firm and lung pressure is high. Singers will naturally strive for the most expressive sound possible, so being able to tell the difference is vital if we are to use our voices economically.

Leakage is not the same as "breathy". According to my definition leakage is involuntary whereas breathy is deliberate. Singers that naturally sound hoarse may have extra asymmetrical vocal mechanism which leads to incomplete vocal fold closure or irregular vibrations. This gives the singer a certain character which is highly valued in rock, pop and soul. On the other hand it can be straining so it may be appropriate to train the fine motor skills necessary for producing more or less complete closure and for that purpose the nasal consonants is favourable. These exercises may also be used as a vocal warm up.

Exercise no. 18 - Mm [m]

CD
11

Make an [m] sound making it sound the least breathy possible (avoid "hissing")

Exercise no. 19 - Nasal [n]

CD
12

Make an [n] sound, with relaxed jaws.

VOICE REGISTERS

The term voice register refers to notes that share the same type of sound and vibration pattern. This topic is the subject of much discussion in vocal teaching circles. So far vocal coaches, singers, speech therapists and linguists have failed to agree on a standard terminology and over the years around a hundred terms have been introduced. There is perhaps most confusion in the area of vocal teaching, particularly in the rock, pop, and soul genres where the voice is used in ways that aren't covered by traditional definitions. Common terms include speech level singing, chest voice, falsetto register, head voice, modal register, mixed voice, heavy register, light register, registers 1 & 2 and so on.

Singers that have not worked with vocal teachers often simply refer to their "normal" and "high" voices. By normal voice they mean chest register or chest voice, so called because vibrations can be felt in the clavicle (collarbone) when singing loudly in this way. The chest register is the one we associate with our speaking voice; most of us speak in our chest register although there are exceptions particularly amongst women. The term "high" voice refers to the falsetto register. Chest register and falsetto register are the terms I use. Men and women use their voices in the same way when singing rock, pop and soul so I see no reason to use different terminology for each gender.

The audible difference between the chest and falsetto registers is primarily due to the activity of the middle part of the vocal fold muscle (*vocalis*). When it contracts the vocal folds vibrate with a greater mass. The mass of the vocal folds is determined by their length and thickness which means that the difference will be greater in the case of long, thick vocal folds (like men have) than short and thin (like women). This is partly why it is difficult to discern the shift in registers in the female voice and also why their registers are so poorly defined. Opinions differ on what is actually chest register, falsetto register and the area in-between which is sometimes referred to as middle register, mixed register etc. I avoid naming this area and have chosen instead to use terms such as more or less "body", power or weight in the voice. The transition zone is approximately 250-350 Hz (c^1-f^1) for both men and women.

It is important to train in the use of our registers in order to able to finely nuance our performances. You should:

– Expand your chest register in both directions.
– Learn to use your falsetto register even in the middle of your range.
– Equalise or even out the difference between the chest and falsetto registers.
– And last but not least, separate the transition between the registers and make a clear distinction between them.

Chest register

The chest register is our natural speaking register. It is also the most natural register to sing in. Men and women usually encounter different problems when trying to get the most out of their voice registers .Men have a tendency to push too hard in the chest register and risk therefore a forced tone which can lead to fatigue and injury. They usually need to work a little extra in order to make their chest registers less strained. The story is often different for women. Those who have sung a lot as children may have learnt that a woman is expected to chirp prettily which usually means that they use their falsetto register. They are not used to using their chest voice and will have to work on that instead. Training the chest register without straining the vocal folds is particularly challenging especially when working with higher pitches.

To ease up the vocal wear when singing in chest register, you should imagine the feeling of "holding back a laugh" or "retaining a pleasant fragance" you have just inhaled.

Women can locate their chest voices by shouting "Ahoy", "Hello" "No" and such at a comfortable level. Calling out in this way is a natural amplification of the speaking voice and is good way of avoiding going into the falsetto register. It is important to use your body as a source of power and support to avoid forcing the voice. Remember to start at a comfortable pitch when you practice and to shout not scream, although the difference can be fine indeed.

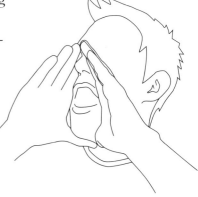

Notfabriken

Exercise no. 20 - "woy"

When practicing slide up to the first note and make sure you start at a comfortable pitch.

Exercise no. 21 - "yeh-yah"

Here it is important not to take in too much air before the phrase starts.

Exercise no. 22 - Sing-a-long "lah"

When doing this exercise try to get your larynx to return to its starting point between each phrase.

A typical rock, pop or soul singer does not produce a singer's formant.

Falsetto register

The falsetto register arises when the vocal fold muscle, *vocalis*, can no longer withstand the force that is stretching the vocal folds. The outer edge starts to vibrate and the vocal folds are stretched hard. When the entire vocalis is no longer contracted the "body" of the note disappears and it become falsetto like or thin. It is logical to conclude that the activity of the vocalis is what gives a note its body although this is yet to be scientifically proven. I even toyed with the idea of calling the chest register the "Vocalis register" but decided that introducing yet another term in this field may simply be adding to the confusion. The falsetto register involves another dominant muscle group, the cricothyroid or CT muscles. This muscle group is the dominant group even at low volumes. In practice one can say that:

– When we sing in *the falsetto register* the CT muscles are especially active.
– When we sing *softly* the CT muscles are especially active.
– When we sing in **the chest register** the vocalis is especially active.
– When we sing **loudly** the vocalis is especially active.

To summarise: In the area of our vocal range where both the chest and falsetto registers can be used it is usually volume that determines which register is dominant.

Men seldom use their falsetto registers. This may be because the falsetto register is perceived as feminine which is usually the last thing boys want to be. Most men only use their falsetto registers when laughing loudly. The falsetto register rarely comes into play in the daily use of their voices and when they begin vocal training they will often try to avoid using it. This is understandable as they don't know how to use it and the sound produced is often unsatisfactory. However, for those who want to develop their singing voice the falsetto register can be a wonderful asset awakening previously unknown nuances and dynamic richness. So for those who are willing to work on it can be well worth the effort. There are many examples of rock, pop and soul singers using this register with great skill. Certain hard rock singers use it when they "scream", something that was particularly popular in the 70's and 80's. However, for most

Notfabriken

of us the falsetto register remains one that is used in combination with the chest register when we feel the need to introduce dynamic nuances.

It is more difficult for women to discern the difference between their registers and therefore when they start vocal training they will need to make quite radical volume shifts particularly in the middle of their range.

Men on the other hand can discern their falsetto register more easily and will also have an easier time bringing it down into the middle of their range. Some singers feel that they use less support when they go from chest register to falsetto register. This is probably due to the fact that lung pressure is usually lower when singing falsetto. Hopefully you will now have at least some idea of the forces involved.

Exercise no. 23 – Falsetto "shEE"

This exercise descends in pitch. It is important to resist the urge to go over to your chest register in the lower part of your range.

If you would like an additional falsetto exercise do exercise no. 61 "OO". Make sure here that you keep to the falsetto register in the middle of your range, ideally by singing softer.

Equalising

Equalising means evening out. In the context of singing it refers primarily to evening out registers, but also vowels as we try to even out the differences between various sounds. In this section we will be dealing with the equalising of registers. We will practice making the shift from chest voice to falsetto inaudible. We can compare equalising with smoothly changing gears while driving. The idea is to do it as smoothly as possible by declutching, easing off the accelerator, engaging the next gear and slowly releasing the clutch pedal. If you are unprepared and untrained you run the risk of sounding like a rooster when you shift registers. In addition to the practical exercise I would like to share two tricks that can help you equalise your registers.

The goal is for the different muscle groups to cooperate and, together with the lung pressure, adjust the volume and airflow.

The first step is to thin out the chest register on the way up so you can shift registers without "breaking". When the shift is approaching pretend that you are about to yawn. This yawning feeling will raise the soft palate and lower the larynx which can make it easier for the laryngeal muscles to cooperate.

My second tip for keeping the body of a note while simultaneously stretching your range upwards is to open your jaws a little extra. This will tilt your larynx and the pitch can be raised that little bit extra. You can then choose whether to sing with a smile or rounded lips. A smile will produce the thinner sound often used by soul singers while rounded lips will produce a fuller, hard rock type of sound. When using these tricks it is essential to control your breathing and use your breathing muscles well.

Exercise no. 24 - Register shift "ah"

CD 17

To locate where your register shifts are located sing a rather loud ascending glissando "ah". When you hear a "rooster" you have shifted registers. Note at which pitch this occurs.

Exercise no. 25 - Equalisation

CD 18

This is where you try to make your register shift inaudible. The further you come down in your range the more chest register you should try to include in the sound. You can make this easier by opening your throat as if yawning when you feel the register shift approaching. Some people find it easier using the same vowel sound throughout the exercise.

Glorious (Andreas Johnson) © EMI Music Publishing Scandinavia AB

Exercise no. 26 - Elastic "dOO"

The point of this exercise is to keep your vocalis slightly contracted. The higher you go up in your range the more you should thin out the sound, without shifting to falsetto. Avoid taking in too much air.

dOO *(on every note)*

Separating

Separating is an expression for purposely making the shift from chest register to falsetto audible and abrupt. This has always been popular in rock, pop and soul but the most extreme form is yodelling! In contrast to equalising, when you want to separate you should sing quite loudly in the chest register all the way to the shift and then "flip" abruptly over. The same method applies when going from falsetto to chest register. The hard part is first relinquishing control and then quickly regaining it to change register and find the right pitch.

To get the most out of this exercise you have to be prepared to sound bad. Learning to separate is hard at first but once mastered will add an exciting dynamic ingredient to your vocals.

49

Exercise no. 27 - Top 5 "now"

This time the shift should be heard. Sing strongly until the shift which occurs on the highest note, it should feel as if it "breaks". This makes it easier to achieve an abrupt shift. The highest note should be sung falsetto and the rest in the chest register.

Exercise no. 28 - Jump off "said I"

CD
21

Performed in the same way as the previous exercise.

Said I loved you but I lied (M. Bolton/R. J. Lange) © Mr Bolton's Music Inc/
Out Of Pocket Prod. Ltd./BMG Music Publishing Scandinavia AB.

Notfabriken

VIBRATO

Vibrato is due to rapid variations in the pitch and, to a lesser degree, the loudness of a note. A static note without vibrato can be perceived as lifeless and unpleasant. A singer can enhance their expression and create dramatic tension by selectively using vibrato. Many people believe that vibrato can bring a song to life in a way that no other technique can.

In classical singing the ideal vibrato is considered to be between five and six undulations per second. A slower vibrato is often associated with older, less elastic voices. Aging produces slower vibrato rate. On the other hand stage fright usually results in fast, uncontrolled undulations with a characteristic "nervous" sound.

Vibrato is within the reach of everyone provided they learn to relax their larynx. The speed and pitch variation of your vibrato is highly individual. It is therefore important to maintain your own personal sound even when it comes to vibrato. A lot of singers would like a more controlled vibrato but to achieve this we need to understand how vibrato works and the factors that influence it.

There are two types of vibrato:

– Natural vibrato
– "Pop" vibrato.

The tempo and pitch variation of natural vibrato varies from singer to singer. It occurs when the vocal fold muscles pulsate. One could also say that natural vibrato is a sign of a relaxed voice and good vocal technique. Pop vibrato however is not necessary a result of relaxation but rather is created by varying your lung pressure to create a pulsating tone that is perceived as a vibrato.

Changing the speed of your natural vibrato is difficult but can be done with practice. Pop vibrato is easily varied so it is tempting to settle for this type alone. This would be a shame as natural vibrato brings another dimension to your singing.

When starting out as a singer it can be difficult to find your natural vibrato, so you may rely on short cuts like shaking your head or flapping your jaw. The only natural way to find your vibrato however is to learn how to relax your jaw and larynx across your entire vocal range. Of course it is harder to relax at the extremities of your range so a lot of practice is required before things loosen up here. It is also worth mentioning that vibrato requires more air – something to bear in mind when planning long notes or phrases.

Now we will work on both natural and pop vibrato.

Exercise no. 29 – Your natural vibrato

CD 22

The entire first part of this exercise is performed without vibrato until you get to the last note "yOO", when you try to relax your larynx. Note that the more you succeed in relaxing the freer your vibrato will be.

A shortcut to achieving natural vibrato is to think about crying. When we cry our larynx tilts allowing the vocal fold muscles to move freely between pitches - something that is necessary for a natural vibrato.

Exercise no. 30 – Pop vibrato

CD 23

Here we will train our breathing muscles to produce variations in lung pressure that resemble vibrato. It may not seem like vibrato at all to begin with, but the faster you get at producing these puffs the more convincing it will become.

VOCAL RIFFING (a.k.a, melisma, licks, turns)

Riffing is vocal ornamentation where the singer makes small changes in the melody. These can either be rehearsed or improvised. Riffing occurs frequently in rock, pop and soul genres with soul in particular making it into an art form. The tendency to riff in certain styles depends upon the prevailing style ideal or the particular abilities or taste of the singer involved. Knowing when, where and how much is vital to achieve the desired effect. Riffing should be used as a spice to enhance your musical expression rather than getting in the way of it.

Here are a few common phrases that can either be used as fixed part of the melody or for finishing off a phrase.

Exercise no. 31 – Basic

CD 24

In this example we do a simple but effective little "skip" which can also form the basis for more advanced figures.

53

Exercise no. 32 - Old School

CD 25

Here we go up first and then down. Don't sing this any faster than you can manage the "pitch shift".

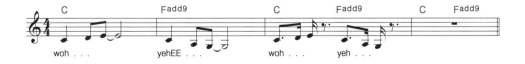

Notfabriken

Singers and musicians often abbreviate short notes and prolong long ones!

Exercise no. 33 – As subtle as a freight train

This one is hard to do but don't give up. Practice makes perfect.

When it comes to vocal riffing there are innumerable variations. The ones presented here were only a few examples.

SUMMARY – VOCAL FOLDS

- The vibrations necessary for the production of sound occur in the vocal folds.
- The vocal folds determine the pitch of the note, which register it is in and whether it is breathy or pressed.
- Your vocal range is the area between the highest and lowest notes you can sing in a controlled manner.
- Long, thick vocal folds produce a lower fundamental frequency, while short, thin ones produce a higher fundamental frequency.
- The onset of a note can take several different forms: hard, breathy, simultaneous or creaky.
- Equalising is a term that refers to the evening out of registers.
- Separating is the term used when making the "break" between chest and falsetto registers abrupt and audible.
- Vibrato is a rapid repetitive variation in pitch and (to a lesser degree) volume.
- There are two types of vibrato: natural and pop.
- More air is needed when the note vibrates.
- The most important thing about vocal riffing is knowing when, where and how much is necessary to achieve the desired effect.

Notfabriken

V: Your sound

Creating your own personal sound is one of the main tasks facing rock, pop and soul singers. Our sound stems from a combination of our physical characteristics and our musical ideals. The physical attributes of singers are probably determined to a small degree by their racial background. For example, one refers to "black" and "white" voices. However, your personal sound is primarily determined by your vocal tract (throat, oral and nasal cavities) so the most efficient way to change your sound is to imitate.

Soprano, alto, tenor and bass are terms derived from classical music for different types of voices and which denote both sound quality and range. It is more difficult to find adequate labels when referring to rock, pop and soul singers as these genres have built their vocal identities on having unique sounds. Songwriters in these styles therefore usually choose key on the basis of the highest possible note. Otherwise, more diffuse descriptions of voice type are used, for example; light voice, clear at high pitches and quite agile or; slightly hoarse, powerful up to G. Sometimes soul singers tend to sound nasal as they rely heavily on their nasal cavity to produce their sound. Rock singers on the other hand may strive for a distorted sound which is achieved by constricting certain structures in the larynx. We may also draw on these techniques to create a sound and expression that reflects our personality or our ideal sound.

The way you perceive a note is coloured by the sound that travels directly from your mouth to your ear, vibrations in your body and how it resonates in the room. All these parameters affect it in different ways. We are often deceived into believing that our voices are deeper than they really are. To get a better idea of how your voice sounds to others you can hold up a large book close to head in front of both ears or cup your hands and hold them about 10 cm in front of your mouth and then speak or sing.

Notice how much higher your voice is? This is close to the way your sound is perceived by others. In order to help you understand your sound we will now look at the factors that influence voice quality.

RESONANCE

To understand why and how we perform the following exercises we need to look at how sound and resonance arise and the factors that affect them.

The fundamentals of resonance:
1. Large rooms produce more bass than small.
2. Hard surfaces (walls, floors etc) reflect more sound, making it appear harder/more powerful.
3. Certain delivery channels propel sound and air better than others and can therefore produce greater volume. Compare your nose to your mouth.

We can develop this idea by comparing your own vocal tract to two very different types of room - the living room and the bathroom. The living room, a large room full of furniture, cushions and curtains, resembles a vocal tract with soft walls in the throat and oral cavity, a low larynx with pouting, rounded lips. Conditions in both the room and the pharynx produce a bass sound due to their size and the soft surfaces that reduce resonance. The bathroom with bare walls, tiles and porcelain fittings can be compared to a tense throat, high larynx and smiling mouth. The sound becomes hard and rich in treble.

Moving your tongue, jaws, soft palate, raising or lowering your larynx, smiling, pouting, tensing or relaxing the walls of your throat or involving your nasal cavities can change your sound completely.

YOUR VOCAL TRACT

Your vocal tract are made up of the various cavities from the vocal folds out to the lips. Resonance occurs in the vocal tract and without it the tone you produce would be nothing but a "buzz". The partials that are produced when your vocal folds vibrate change frequency and intensity for every new pitch and vowel sound. The audio spectrum of an "AH" for example is quite different from that of an "EE".

Your vocal tract affect many aspects of your sound and are therefore of great interest to singers. We can colour our vowels to enable the audience to understand what we sing, we can shape our sound to reflect our personality and musical ideals and increase the perceived volume.

Most singers want to be able to sing loudly and even if this is primarily a function of lung pressure, using your vocal tract to best effect can help. A trained singer can produce more efficient voice pulses than an untrained one which creates better material to resonate. This is because their overall vocal technique has been refined to a point where everything from breathing to articulation works better. Continued training usually leads to an increase in volume as well.

YOUR EQUALISER

You can compare the larynx, throat, nasal and oral cavities to your stereo's graphic equalizer. Changing the settings changes the sound. Here are several factors that affect your sound from vocal folds to the final note.

– Register is determined by the vibration pattern of the vocal folds. You can choose to sing in the chest or falsetto register.

– The glottal adduction determines how breathy, flowy or pressed the sound is.

– The larynx may be placed in a low, neutral or high position. Lowering your larynx extends your vocal tract resulting in a deeper, more resonant sound, while raising it has the opposite effect.

- The vestibular folds (false vocal folds) and the arytenoid cartilage can be constricted to produce a distorted sound.

- The walls of the throat can be tensed or relaxed. A tense throat results in hard walls that enhance resonance while a relaxed throat decreases resonance.

- The soft palate can be raised or lowered resulting in more or less resonance from the nasal cavities. This determines how nasal the sound will be.

- The tongue is probably the most flexible structure in your tract. You can lay it flat in your mouth, curl the front or back of it, tense or relax it, all of which will affect your sound.

- Your lips can be rounded or stretched into a smile. Rounded or putting lips extend your space resulting in a deeper sound. A smile will produce more treble.

So, there are obviously a lot of parameters to keep track of in the quest for your ideal sound. Remember that the partials that you have worked hard on developing can be dialed out or enhanced with one movement of a recording engineer's hand. This can be both good and bad but it is something you should definitely be aware of when dealing with engineers as you may have to make some adjustments.

VOWELS

In order to produce as even an audio experience as possible for the listener and access those exquisitely placed partials that enrich your sound. You should concentrate on directing the sound to the hard, resonant space at the front of your mouth. You will have to place the tip of your tongue behind the bottom front teeth and raise the back of your tongue. Certain vowels such as "EE" are naturally formed in this way, however you will have to modify others such as "AH".

A singer's maximum lung pressure is 30-60 cm VP, whereas a glass blower can reach 250 cm VP!

Exercise no. 34 – The natural sound of vowels

CD 27

First we will find out how vowels sound before being modified.

Exercise no. 35 - Back to front "lEEih"

CD 28

In this exercise you will try to direct all vowels to the front part of your mouth. This is best done by placing the top of the tip of your tongue behind your lower front teeth and then pronouncing the vowels by lifting the rest of your tongue as required.

DIPHTHONGS

A diphthong is where you glide between two vowel sounds without an interceding consonant. This is common when rock, pop and soul singers form their sounds. Some of the most common diphthongs are:

"ey", "ay", "oy", "ow".

Notfabriken

Exercise no. 36 - Diphthongs

Sound the entire diphthong in the one place by placing the tip of your tongue behind your lower front teeth. When you've mastered this, try separating the diphthongs as much as possible and note the effect it has on your sound.

VOICE QUALITIES AND IDEALS

There are innumerable voice qualities and ideals. An ideal in itself is often a combination of several other ideals. When an ideal appears it is analysed by singing teachers and vocal coaches who define and describe how to reproduce it. As previously mentioned the best way to achieve a particular sound is by imitation. Singing along with singers whose sound you like will help you work out what to do. If this doesn't' work you can always consult a teacher who will map out how to create the sound and a method for learning it. The range of ideals and techniques is enormous and the terms used for them are usually fairly descriptive, for example growling and crooning. However, as vocal pedagogy in the rock, pop and souls genres is relatively new, there is much discussion as to which terms and methods should be used. For example this book is an attempt to consolidate my subjective experience into a body of theory. However, we have a long way to go before we have arrived at a universally accepted and homogenous nomenclature for vocal expression. Below is a list of some of the most common expressions and vocal ideals. I would like to point out that the artists mentioned often, but not *always*, use the named techniques.

Belting

Belting is often used in rock, pop and soul as well as in musical theatre. Belting is really an expression for *energetic singing*. The technique

Notfabriken

is characterised by high lung pressure, high pitch and volume with an elevated larynx. The name stems from the expression to "belt out". Belting occurs in the upper part of the chest register.

Exercise no. 37 – Test belt "uh-oh"

– Inhale a little air.
– Hold your neck straight and look up.
– Close your vocal folds.
– Shout "uh-oh" quite loudly, as if something bad was about to happen.

Artists who use this technique:
Alanis Morrisette; Björk, Celine Dion, Michael Bolton, Dave Grohl (Foo Fighters); Freddie Mercury (Queen)

You can also think of exercises 20, 21 and 22 on page 45 in terms of belting.

Twang

Twang is a technique that colours your sound through the liberal production of overtones. The classic American accent is a good example of "twang" and this sound is used by singers in a wide variety of styles. Twang sounds like kids teasing each other by saying "na,na,na,na,na,na". Some voice professionals believe that twang is the result of the contraction of the aryepiglottic sphincter.

Artists:
Anastacia, Shania Twain, Joss Stone, Chris Robinson(Black Crowes), Usher

You can also think of exercise 41 on page 68 in terms of twang.

Singers usually pitch big jumps upwards too high and big jumps down too low!

Growl and Distortion

"Growling" is exactly that - growling. Growling is mostly restricted to certain types of hard rock although a "lighter" version can be found in other genres. Growling uses high lung pressure, a constricted larynx and low pitch.

Distortion is used in both rock and hard rock either as temporary effect or throughout a song. In contrast to growling, distortion almost always occurs at high pitch, with high lung pressure and that leads to vibration in the parts of the larynx above the vocal folds.

Artists:
Growl: *Lou Koller (Sick of it); Peter Dolving (The Haunted)*

Distortion: *Bonnie Tyler, Janis Joplin; Anouk; Brian Johnson (AC/DC), Bryan Adams, Udo Dirkschneider (Accept; U.D.O)*

Exercise no. 38 – Distortion

CD
30

Some singers, particularly women, have trouble producing a distorted tone and others get a sore throat when trying. If this happens you should stop, rest your voice and try again later. It is important that your body language and attitude is energetic.

– Place the tip of your tongue behind your lower front teeth and smile!
– Place the sides of the rear of your tongue against your upper canine teeth.
– Using high lung pressure, make a prolonged "ey", "mEE" or "ahOO" sound.
– Now your tone should be distorted.

If you don't produce a distorted sound, try again until you find the right combination of "settings". Remember that it requires a lot of lung pressure and energy to sound distorted. If you produced a good sound but your throat hurt you will need to make small adjustments with your tongue and soft palate. Train for short periods of time and stop as soon as you feel discomfort.

If the above methods don't work try tuning in to an extreme emotional state such as rage.

Making generalisations and mapping how a rock, pop or soul singer sings is difficult and the exceptions are many. Nevertheless I will now try to briefly describe the most common types of voices in their respective genres.

Rock

Rock singers usually sing at high pitches, with high lung pressure, using their chest register with little or no vibrato and distortion as an effect.

Artists:
Ann Wilson (Heart), Avril Lavigne, Bruce Springsteen, Chris Cornell (Soundgarden, Audioslave), Bono (U2)

Pop

Pop is usually sung at a comfortable pitch, with moderate lung pressure and often with a light and/or breathy tone. Vibrato is used sparingly and creaky onsets and glottal stops are common phrasing devices.

Artists:
Madonna, Britney Spears, Nina Persson (Cardigans), Ronan Keating, Chris Martin (Coldplay), Beck.

Soul

The soul singer chooses key with a view to being able to use the whole of their vocal range. Once again we have moderate lung pressure, switching from twangy to breathy and a wide vibrato. The soul singer can at times be perceived as nasal. Glottal stops, prolonged nasal offsets and improvised riffing are all important ingredients.

Artists:
Mary J. Blige, Lauryn Hill, Brandy, Stevie Wonder, Brian McKnight, John Legend

Traditional hard rock

There is a style within hard rock where singers (especially men) sing extremely high but with a powerful, resonant sound. This sound is characterised by high lung pressure, neutral to lowered larynx, wide vibrato and open vowels. No research has been carried out on this type of singing so any attempts at analysis are simply conjecture. Some claim that the falsetto register is used while others insist that the chest register is dominant.

Artists:

Bruce Dickinson (Iron Maiden), Rob Halford (Judas Priest)

Exercise no. 39 - Hard rock "oh"

CD
31

Round your lips while opening your mouth as if you were holding a hot potato in it. Keep your larynx neutral and take deep breaths before each phrase. Imagining that you are on the verge of crying can also help you to relax on the high notes. Try the sound "UH" as well.

64

SUMMARY - SOUND

– Your vocal tract include all the cavities that exist between the vocal folds and the lips.

– Your personal sound depends on the shape of your cavities, but also upon your lingual characteristics and accent.

– The best way to learn a sound is to copy it.

– The terms soprano, alto, tenor and bass are derived from classical singing and describe both range and sound colour.

– Large rooms result in more bass.

– Hard walls are more reflective and result in sound being perceived as harder/louder.

– A large sound channel such as the mouth can produce greater volumes than a small one such as the nasal cavity.

– Your larynx, throat, nasal/oral cavities can be compared with a stereo's graphic equalizer.

– A diphthong arises when you change vowel sound without an interceding consonant.

– Growling may be sung in low keys.

– Distortion is used in both rock and hard rock, either as a temporary effect or for whole songs. In contrast to growling, distortion is almost always used at high pitch.

Notfabriken

Whispering can make you sound secretive!

Repetition is the key to learning. *Unknown*

VI: Articulation

To articulate means to pronounce words and phrases clearly, however articulation is also a musical tool. Both vowels and consonants can be used expressively, but in general I would say that the pitch of vowels convey feelings while consonants give the lyrics clarity. If you articulate clearly the audience will stand a better chance of grasping the lyrics and this will naturally add another dimension to your musical expression. Your "articulators" mould your consonants and changing their shape, position or density can make a big difference to your sound. A singer's articulators are his or her:

– Lips
– Tongue
– Lower jaw
– Soft palate

Articulation of vowels is dealt with in the chapter Sound. We will now look at the articulation of consonants.

CONSONANTS

In addition to their lyrical function consonants can also be a rhythmic ingredient. Explosive consonants create a percussive element that can be used to great effect and really make things swing. In my opinion the roll of consonants in musical interpretation is underrated. This may be due to the fact that traditional teachers are a little scared of consonants because the way they constrict a tone can lead to tension or voice wear.

Notfabriken

Even when the consonant is formed with the tongue and teeth there is a tendency to close the glottis at the same time. It is important that singers are made aware of this so they can avoid falling into the habit and wearing out their voices.

A singer should develop ability to move between different articulator positions. When a consonant is formed air flow is stopped or constricted. It is therefore important not to dwell too long on the consonant as this can create tension in the structures that are forming it.

The pitch of a vowel is determined during the formation of the preceding consonant. Some consonants lowers the pitch a little and much of the energy disappears into the throat instead of out the mouth. This is why consonants should be formed lightly and explosively.

It is important to remain relaxed during the following exercises. You may notice that you begin to tense your jaw muscles after a while.

Exercise no. 40 - Fat lip [b],[p],[m]

CD
32&33

A/ This is where we train our labial consonants i.e. those formed with our lips. Make sure you relax your lips after every consonant.

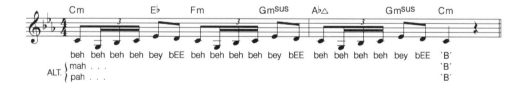

B/ This is similar to the preceding exercise instead here we train all the labial consonants in one exercise.

beh beh beh beh bey bEE, pah   pah pah pah pah pah,   mah mah mah mah mah mah 'B'

Start off at a comfortable tempo but work on increasing the speed of the exercise. Feel free to use a metronome so you can chart your progress. Make sure you maintain an even rhythm. Try setting the metronome at the fastest speed at which you can do [m] – the most difficult of the consonants in the group.

Exercise no. 41 - [n],[l],[t],[d]

CD
34&35

This is where we train the consonants that are formed with the tip of the tongue and alveolar ridge.

A/ Relax your jaw and shoulders and try to perform this exercise in a relaxed and rhythmic way.

nah . . . nah...(on every note)

ALT. { lah . . .
tah . . .
dah . . .

The Look (Per Gessle) © Jimmy Fun Music

B/ The same melody as above, but now we will include other consonants. Adjust your tempo to as fast as you can do [d].

nah . . .   lah . . .   tah . . .   dah . . .   nah . . .

(nah). . .

Exercise no. 42 – Latino [g], [k], 'ng'

Now it's time for the consonants that are formed by the tongue and soft palate.

A/ Same instructions as in the previous exercise. Relax your jaws and facial muscles and perform the exercise lightly and rhythmically.

gih   koh . . .

B/ Once again we conclude this group of consonants by putting them all together.

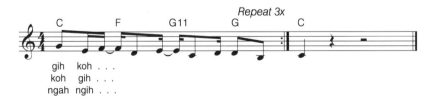

gih   koh . . .
koh   gih . . .
ngah ngih . . .

Notfabriken

"Covering" a note is a way of modifying the vowel so it is more comfortable to sing. An "ah" can be sung more like an "AH"

THE JAWS

Jaw movement is not only vitally important for all types of singing, it is also central to a wide range of activities including chewing, grinding your teeth and the formation of formants, vowels and consonants. The movements of the jaw often follow those of the tongue with the exception of certain vowels such as when moving form "EE" to "OO". The jaw muscles contract every time you close your mouth, so it is important not only to avoid clenching your jaws but also to allow gravity to help you to open your mouth. Some teachers recommend keeping your jaw still and letting your tongue do most of the work forming consonants, however I believe that the jaw is a natural part of sound formation and that tension in the jaw muscles can be avoided by keeping the jaws moving. It also seems to help rhythmic articulation.

Stress and anxiety often cause us to unconsciously clench our jaws, which leads to tense jaw muscles. This can also result in tension in the larynx and subsequent vocal wear. Pressing your tongue against the hard palate or clenching your jaws can often occur when performing daily activities such as watching TV or walking. This also causes your mouth and throat to assume their swallowing positions which creates extra tension which can lead to problems with your mucosa. Jaw clenching can also create tension in your neck and temples resulting in headaches. Relaxing your jaws should be practiced when performing. Voice massage can relieve built-up tension however the problem will return if your technique doesn't improve. Keeping this warning in mind, here is a suggestion for avoiding unnecessary tension.

The basic position for a relaxed jaw is as follows: tip of your tongue behind your lower front teeth, lips sealed, jaws slightly open. If you place your fingers at the back of your jaw and open your mouth you will be able to observe the jaw's natural movement pattern. You will feel the jawbone move down and then backwards.

Notfabriken

The following exercises should be performed while relaxed and with a feeling of mobility in the jaw.

Exercise no. 43 – The classic "vEE-vEE"

Perform this exercise lightly.

It is a good idea to keep your fingers on the back of your jaw when performing all of these exercises. This will help you get a sense of the mobility that is required to remain relaxed. If after a while your jaw becomes tense or tired, rest and give yourself some voice massage.

Exercise no. 44 – Hold out "vah"

This exercise is extremely tiring. The short breathing pauses and rapid jaw movements will tire you out quickly and you will be forced to relax to complete the exercise. This will develop your ability to control the technique which will help to you perform for longer periods.

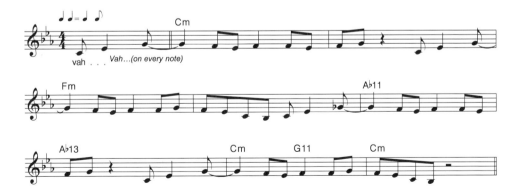

Exercise no. 45- Gospel "woh"

This exercise should be performed with a sense of unbridled joy! Let the first syncopated notes help your voice to sing the ascending figure more easily.

SUMMARY - ARTICULATION

- Articulation refers to pronouncing words and phrases clearly, but is also a musical tool.

- Explosive consonants create a percussive element that can help the singer to swing.

- The pitch of a vowel is determined during the formation of the preceding consonant.

- It is important not to dwell too long on consonants as you may tense up and increase the wear on your voice.

- Stress and poor vocal habits can create tension in the jaw muscles resulting in vocal wear.

The meaning of life is long term happiness.
Dalai Lama

VII: Swingin' it

As a singer, the ability to "swing" can make all the difference. Unfortunately this aspect is often neglected, which is strange considering that rhythm is actually the musical foundation on which harmonies and melodies are built. Rock, pop and soul have evolved primarily out of the Afro-American tradition where rhythm is one of the main ingredients. When African slaves were transported to America, two separate musical directions developed, both of which had their origins in the African rhythmic tradition. South African slaves played various percussion instruments and through instruments such as the congas and tambourine developed the complex rhythms we see in Latin American music. The slaves in North America were forbidden to play instruments which meant that their rhythmic tradition developed through song. "Call and response" work songs formed the basis of the blues and Negro spirituals developed into gospel. Gospel was taken out of the church and became soul. Aspects of the English ballad tradition were also involved and went on via country music to be mixed with blues and eventually turn into rock. This cycle of development has continued up to the present day resulting in a plethora of multifaceted styles that defy categorisation.

The fact that Afro-American style rhythm is often neglected in vocal training may be a question of culture. People in regions with a different musical heritage may feel unsure as to how to incorporate it into their singing. Another reason may be that using the types of note onsets, offsets and consonants that enhance the rhythm of a song can be vocally wearing. As I have said before, we singers should not let technical hurdles stand in the way of our vocal expression. We simply have to train singing rhythmically until it becomes less tiring. In this chapter we will examine rhythmic expression and ask the question "How can you get your vocals to swing?"

Notfabriken

One seldom sees a singer of gospel or any other rhythmic style stand still when they sing. Rhythm is also expressed through movement so it is vital that the rhythmic element of a song is also firmly rooted in the body. There are various elements that can be worked on to achieve this, but a good way to start is by focusing on the rhythmic aspects when listening to or playing music. Listen to the drums, how any other percussion instruments are played and the rhythmic phrasing of the bass. This will create an increased awareness that will help you as a singer. Singers that have played drums or bass are often better at making a song swing simply because they are more aware of the rhythmic aspects. Being rhythmically aware heightens your overall musicality.

You should perform the following exercises with a metronome, something that is also useful in many of the situations a singer experiences. The elements we will be training are:

Keeping time
Having a solid feel for the tempo of a song will make it easier to deviate from or follow it when expressing yourself rhythmically.

Coordination
The ability to coordinate your voice with the rest of your body is important and will help you to liberate the rhythmic properties of your body and voice.

Timing
Knowing how to accentuate rhythmic undercurrents is important.

KEEPING TIME

Keeping time means being able to feel and maintain a given tempo. Tempo reflects the energy of a song and can therefore say a lot. Tempo can change or remain constant. Constant tempo is most common in rock, pop and soul, often slowing down at the end of a song. The unit used to measure tempo is Bpm (beats per minute). In order to develop your ability to get the feel of, recognise and maintain a constant tempo you can train in the following way.

Exercise no 46 - Keeping time

CD
41, 42
43

The example below is sung with a reprise, which means singing it all the way through twice. The entire melody is demonstrated first and then you are given the chance to sing it through once before the exercise starts again. The piano will accompany you for the first four bars and then you will sing without accompaniment until the final two bars where the piano comes in again. In the reprise you will sing unaccompanied until the final two bars. In this way you will be able to see if your singing was in time with the reappearance of the metronome.

A Common time (4/4) Bpm: 110

B Common time (4/4) Bpm: 150

C Common time (4/4) Bpm: 60

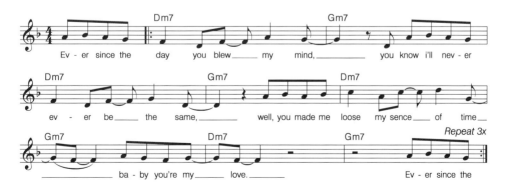

COORDINATION

Being able to coordinate your voice and body is very important. Singers are often called upon to be conductors at the beginning and end of songs which means they will need to be well coordinated. Coordination will also enhance your rhythmic awareness and freedom.

- Stamping your foot. The basis of polyrhythm along with clapping.
- Clapping: The basis of polyrhythm together with stamping your foot.
- Singing: Singing is performed with maximum swing and precision without being affected by the stamping and clapping.

Exercise no. 47 - Fonky

CD
44

Listen to the CD first and then practice with a metronome, set at a slow tempo until you have the timing "nailed".

Bpm: 85

Exercise no. 48 – Happy Birthday

CD
45

Performed as above.

Bpm: 120

Happy Birthday (Stevie Wonder) © Jobete Music Co Inc/Black Bull Music Inc.
För Norden: EMI Music Publishing Scandinavia AB.

Exercise no. 49 - Singer

Once again, same pattern as previously.

Bpm 80

Original lyrics: I was born an original sinner I was born from original sin.

Missionary Man (A. Lennox/D. A. Stewart) © D 'N' A Ltd/BMG Music Publishing Scandinavia AB

TIMING

Some people are blessed with naturally good timing and others have to work hard at it. Frank Sinatra was known for his timing as is Stevie Wonder. Timing is essential to all improvisation and harmony singing where the ability to listen and react quickly is a must. Timing involves finding the right note value and then creatively interpreting the beginning and ends of notes in a way that works with the accompaniment. You may choose to sing slightly before, after or right on the given note value. The basis of good timing is the ability to feel the rhythmic pulse and to keep time. There are an infinite number of possible rhythmic combinations but here are a few basic note values you can practice with.

Exercise no. 50 - Half notes

Listen to the example of the CD and then practice on your own with a metronome.

Bpm 70

Exercise no. 51 – Quarter notes

CD 48

Here we work on quarter note timing.

Bpm 70

Exercise no. 52 – Eighth note "off beat"

CD 49

Here we work on "off beat" timing.

Bpm 70

Exercise no. 53 – Sixteenth notes

CD 50

Sixteenth notes timing.

Bpm 70

Exercise no. 54 – Triplets

CD 51

Triplets are also used in rock, pop and soul.

Bpm 70

Notfabriken

GHOST NOTES

Ghost notes are often used by musicians, especially drummers. These are subtle percussive elements that are played or sung in between the ordinary notes. Guitarists may strike muted strings or a drummer may throw in an extra, light snare beat. Where ghost notes are concerned the key word is "subtle".

Singers don't use ghost notes as often, which may depend upon lack of training, ability or fear of straining their voice. A sung ghost note consists of a weak glottal attack where the vocal folds are slammed together. This can cause fatigue. Michael Jackson is one singer that frequently uses ghost notes, to the point that they have become a trademark sound. The basis of creating extra swing with ghost notes is good timing in conjunction with other rhythmic elements.

There are no ghost note exercises presented here as these should be practiced under the watchful eye of a teacher who can help you avoid straining your voice. The basic technique however is presented in Exercise no.16 on page 41.

SUMMARY - SWINGIN' IT

- Rhythm is one of the main ingredients of rock, pop and soul.
- The type of onsets and offsets that enhance the rhythmic qualities of a song can cause vocal strain but are nevertheless a useful vocal element.
- Rhythmic expression must be rooted in the body, not just the voice.
- A solid feel for the given tempo of a song will allow you greater freedom when improvising rhythmically.
- The ability to coordinate your voice and body will help you free up your rhythmic potential.
- Keeping time refers to the ability to feel and maintain a given tempo.
- Timing is essential to all improvisation and harmony singing where the ability to listen and react quickly is a must.
- Timing involves finding the right note value and then creatively interpreting onsets and offsets in a way that works with the accompaniment.
- Ghost notes are subtle percussive elements that are played or sung in between the ordinary notes.

He who knows not what there is to know does not understand what's missing
Rolf Christersson

VIII. The gig

The gig, be it an audition or a concert, is the place where all your training and artistic vision is supposed to come to fruition. This is where you interpret musical signals and where your voice and the music unite convey emotion and tell stories. Hopefully the audience will be treated to the entertainment experience they were expecting and you will receive the artistic recognition you deserve. You won't always love the material you present, nor will it always be artistically satisfying or challenging. However you can always find some satisfaction in the fact that the audience went home one musical experience the richer.

The purpose of vocal training is to allow you to interpret lyrics and music more fully while keeping your voice in good enough shape to be able to perform as often as you like.

The way a song is expressed depends on the composer's intention, the character of the song and the way you choose to perform it. However, before we are able to perform or record we must first learn the material, interpret it and generally prepare for the gig.

Your credibility when performing a song is vital. To be credible it is essential that you have taken in the lyrics and music and decided upon a particular interpretation.
Interpretation can be divided into two aspects:

LYRICS

The main task of a singer is to be able to convey the feelings or message contained in the lyrics. In cases where the lyrics are nonsensical one needs to emphasise the musical interpretation.

Many lyrics contain double meanings which gives the singer a certain freedom of interpretation. The first step in interpreting a song is:

Read the lyrics:
– Are there any words you don't understand? Look them up.
– What is the song about? Is there any ambiguity?
– Can you personally relate to the lyrics?
– What would you like to convey through the lyrics?

The next step is to create a mental picture of the environment in which the song's story takes place. This will enhance your ability to understand and convey its message and express it vocally and through movement and facial expressions.

Surroundings – Where does the plot unfold?
– Is it indoors or outdoors?
– Is it day or night?
– Is it raining or sunny?
– What season is it?
– Is it in town or in the country?

Historical period
– What did things look like at the time the song's story takes place?

Who are you?
– Are you the narrator or the main character?
– Are you a man or a woman?
– Where do you come from?
– What's your background and social standing?
– How educated are you and what do you do for a living?

The senses – what sensory experiences do you have in the story?
– What do you see?
– What do you hear?
– How do things smell?
– What can you taste?

– How do you feel?
– What are the dominant colours?
– What do you fantasise about?

When you've come this far it is time to think about how you can convey the scene you have created for the lyrics.

Emotional states- Close your eyes for a few minutes and reflect on how you are when you are:
– Happy
– Alert
– In love
– Disappointed
– Angry
– Hurt
– Elated
– Tired
– Contemplative
– Irritated
– Indifferent

Body language- How does your body react in response to each feeling?
– What is your posture like?
– Do you sit or stand?
– Do you stand still or move around?
– How do you move?

Facial expressions – Which faces do you associate with each emotional state?
– Which facial expressions are included?
– How do you use your eyes? What sort of look is required?

Notfabriken

Swollen mucosa produce sticky mucous!

Vocals – Which sound and musical elements can enhance the prevailing feeling?
– Loud or soft notes?
– Falsetto or chest voice?
– Pressed or breathy sound?
– Staccato or legato phrasing?

Exercise no. 55 - Moods

Sing a song of your choice but vary the mood in which you sing. Note the different results.

Learning lyrics by heart

Learning lyrics on short notice can be a problem. When you are forced to learn lyrics quickly you will be unable to interpret them as methodically as we just did. The important thing is to remember key words that jog your memory. A few tips:

– Write the lyrics down. If you already have a written or printed copy, copy them by hand again!
– Memorise the first word of every new part of the song e.g. verse and chorus!
– Memorise the first word of every phrase!

THE MUSIC

Interpreting the music in a way that satisfies both the composer and the artist before the gig is a must. You should be so determined and finely nuanced that no type of vocal expression is beyond you. Only then will you be truly free to interpret musical messages. The path to total vocal freedom is of course endless, but this should not deter you from continually striving to develop.

Musical signals for the singer can take the form of:
– Tempo
– Key
– Beat
– Harmony
– Melody
– Rhythm
– Instrumental elements

All of these ingredients can help you to choose:
– Register
– Sound
– Articulation
– Dynamics
– Phrasing
– Timing
– Intensity

Just as for the interpretation and learning of lyrics, music can also have an underlying motif. Quick tempo, major harmonies and short phrases can imply staccato phrasing. You should also exploit all the nuances we look at in the other chapters dealing with vocal technique, especially those concerning register, sound and rhythm.

DYNAMICS

Dynamics is concerned with movement and change. Changes in a song's rhythm, power and melody add emotional nuances and enhance the listeners understanding of the lyrics. Dynamics can create musical tension which helps to capture the audience's attention. In music theory the term dynamics is used to refer to variations in volume, however I would like to give it a broader meaning.

The musical elements that can be perceived as changes in dynamics are:

– Accents
– Note values
– Pitch
– Volume
– Sound
– Articulation
– Vibrato

Exercise no. 56 – Lyrical dynamics

This exercise is a short example of what we talked about when looking at the interpretation of lyrics and music. Here we take a short, nonsensical phrase, split it in two and interpret it vocally. We interpret "Sweet love turned cold" by taking "Sweet love" and singing it tenderly and legato in the falsetto register, and then giving "Turned cold" a harder, colder interpretation by singing it loudly, staccato and in the chest register. This is a highly simplified way of interpreting a lyric, but can nevertheless give you an indication of how you can bring lyrics to life through simple dynamic changes.

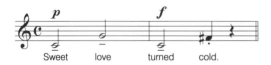

THE HOUR IS UPON YOU

Now we come to the actual performance. After having carefully worked through the material we now have an extremely good chance of treating the audience to a satisfying musical experience. In order to get the most out of this experience and to be able to perform to the best of your ability on that given day, there are a few other factors that you will need to consider. First we will look at how to deal with the array of feelings that usually appear before a gig.

Nerves

Being nervous prior to a gig is a natural part of the situation. In fact, the adrenalin surge that accompanies pre-gig nerves is often beneficial, heightening your awareness and focus, sharpening your senses and improving your reaction times. So far, so good. But what happens when your nerves take over to the point where you become paralysed with fear? We become nervous because we are afraid of not being able to live up to the expectations we believe other people have of us. I would like to distinguish between nerves and fear.

- Nerves. Where the nervousness is positive and can lead to enhanced performance.
- Fear. Where nerves spill over into fear and can have dire consequences.

Fear is a primal reaction inherited from our cavemen ancestors, developed in response to the daily threat of winding up on some predator's menu. The body responds to being nervous and being afraid in the same way. The only difference is the amount of the chemicals secreted and our ability to control our reactions. One reaction can be a dry mouth, tense muscles, hyperventilation or butterflies in your stomach. In addition, vital muscles in the larynx contract affecting our vocal control. This results in fatigue that prevents your voice from reaching its full potential.

So what can we do to stop out thoughts running away with us so that we only experience the positive effects of nerves? Sensitivity naturally varies from person to person but here are a few tips that can help you control your reactions.

Exercise no. 57 - Visualising the performance

Visualise the entire situation on the morning of the day of the performance.
- Sit comfortably, make sure things are quiet around you and close your eyes!
- Run through the whole gig in real time including between song patter.

Notfabriken

- What does the gig venue look like?
- Who do you think will be there?
- Where will the people you know in the audience sit?
- Imagine the ideal performance where everything you do works perfectly!
- After this visualisation it may be time to warm up, calmly and methodically!
- If you aren't in the best shape today, accept this and trust that it will still be good enough!
- Do not strain your voice for the rest of the day!

Exercise no. 58 - Composing yourself

Here we will be using the breathing exercises from the chapter Breathing/Breathing for relaxation (Refer to Exercise no.15)

- Place your right index and middle fingers between your eyebrows
- Place your thumb and ring finger on either side of your nostrils
- Close one nostril with your thumb and breathe deeply and slowly through the other one
- Close the other nostril with your ring finger and repeat the breathing pattern through the open nostril
- Close your eyes and repeat calmly for two minutes

More tips for the gig:
- Make sure you're ready in time, including clothes and makeup so that this won't add to your stress
- Make sure everything you need on stage is there in time: water, towels etc
- Both your clothes and between song patter should be well prepared and reflect both the music and the audience!

Making an entrance

You only have one chance to make a first impression at a gig or an audition. In addition you usually only have a limited time on stage so you can hardly expect the audience to get to know you're hidden qualities. A few things to think about:

– Take a deep breath and walk assertively on stage!
– If you haven't seen the venue before (e.g. in the case of auditions) quickly ascertain where you have to stand!
– Regard the audience with a steady gaze!
– Adjust the microphone stand or remove the microphone if it suits you!
– If it is a concert you will naturally look at individuals in the audience, however at auditions it is better to focus on a point somewhere else in the room. Staring the judging panel in the face is uncomfortable and unnatural.
– If you need to instruct the accompanist, be clear and concise. Be well prepared and perhaps even have a metronome with you to dictate the tempo. Good luck!

Notfabriken

SUMMARY - THE GIG

- The gig, be it an audition or a concert, is the place where all your training and artistic vision is supposed to come to fruition.

- Dynamics is concerned with movement and change.

- The adrenalin surge that accompanies pre-gig nerves is often beneficial, heightening your awareness and focus, sharpening your senses and improving your reaction time.

- We become nervous because we are afraid of not being able to live up to the expectations we believe other people have of us.

- Fear is a primal reaction inherited from our cavemen ancestors, developed in response to the daily threat of winding up on some predator's menu.

- If you aren't in the best shape today, accept this and trust that it will still be good enough!

- Make sure you're ready in time, including clothes and makeup so that this won't add to your stress.

- You only have one chance to make a first impression at a gig or an audition.

Notfabriken

IX: After the gig

When the gig is over your adrenalin is flowing and the muscles in your larynx are well supplied with blood, lubricated and stretched. The larynx will often move up slightly after you have sung for a while which means that the vocal folds are stretched more than is usual for your speaking voice and your voice will be higher. Talking at this higher pitch can wear your voice out. The liberal flow of blood to the vocals folds can lead to swelling of the vocal folds or mucosa when they cool down. As is true of all physical activity it is important to stretch the muscle fibres so that they don't stiffen and can return to their original condition as quickly as possible.

The possibility of post-gig voice care varies from situation to situation, but it is important that you give yourself five minutes after every gig. If there is no where you can be alone go into the rest room.

WINDING DOWN

Winding down means lowering your pulse, slowing down your breathing and reducing adrenalin levels.

Exercise no. 59 - Breathing out

To slow our breathing down we use the breathing exercise described in the section of Breathing/Breathing for relaxation (Refer to Exercise no.15 on page 38)

– Place the index and middle finger of your right hand between your eyebrows.
– Place your thumb and ring finger over your nostrils.
– Close one nostril with your thumb and breathe in deeply and calmly through the other nostril.
– Release your thumb, close the other nostril with your ring finger and breathe in deeply and calmly.
– Close your eyes and repeat the exercise slowly for two minutes.

Exercise no. 60 - Stretching

To stretch we use the exercises we performed in the chapter *Warming up.*

A/ Neck
(For an illustration refer to exercise no. 3 A on page 20)

– Slowly tilt your head to the left. Breathe.
– Tilt your head to the right. Breathe.
– Lift your head back up to its normal position.
– Place your hands on your collarbones and pull downwards.
– Slowly tilt your head backwards while opening your mouth. Jut your bottom jaw out (as if you had an underbite) 3-5 times.
– Let your head fall slowly forward until your chin is almost resting on your chest (don't force it) Breathe.

C/Back
(For an illustration refer to exercise no. 3 C on page 20)

– Interlock your fingers behind your back and push your chest out. Breathe in.
– Push your hips forward and then stretch your back like a cat. Breathe out.
– Repeat.

Notfabriken

VOCAL COOL DOWN

Cooling down is a process that includes stretching of the vocal folds and relaxing the larynx. This is vital to avoid vocal fold swelling after intensive voice use.

CD
53

Exercise no. 61 - Back to square one "OO".

Begin by singing softly in the falsetto register. Then let the chest register take over as you progress further down in your range. Sing softly all the time.

SUMMARY - AFTER THE GIG

– The liberal flow of blood to the vocals folds after a gig can lead to swelling of the vocal folds or mucosa when they cool down. As is true of all physical activity it is important to stretch the muscle fibres so that they can return to their original position as quickly as possible.

– Give yourself five minutes alone after every gig. If there is no where you can be alone, go into the toilet.

– Winding down means lowering your pulse, slowing down your breathing and reducing adrenalin levels.

– To avoid vocal fold swelling it is important that you cool down.

The glottal wave moves from the bottom up!

X: A few words about ...

A DAY IN THE LIFE OF A SINGER

Many's the singer that has found themselves with a fever and painfully inflamed throat just half and hour before a gig and thought "OK. Now what?" Or experienced the icy hand of panic clutch their hearts when they realise that their voice is shot just three songs onto a gig. The reason for this anxiety may be the prevailing "pitch hysteria" in the music business. By this I mean that singers are sometimes forced to sing at extremely high pitches regardless of their natural pitch and physical characteristics. Obviously if someone is forced time and time again to sing numerous choruses at the top of their range their voice will give out. No one in their right mind would expect a hundred meters runner to maintain top speed for ten kilometres! Another cause of anxiety is that your voice is extremely dependent on your general physical and mental well-being. Negative stress, worry, colds, lacks of sleep all affect our vocal abilities and as these things can change from day to day a singer's life can be plagued by uncertainty.

"Fighting the bull" is an expression often used to describe a singer's roll both onstage and off as leader of a band, a solo artist or leading roll in a musical. The expression reflects the fact that the audience often focuses on the singer even if the entire ensemble contributes to creating the show. Obviously it is difficult to hold the attention of an audience if your voice is shot. In order for a singer to give a good performance it is essential that the other musicians are sensitive to his or her requirements. If a singer feels that their voice is in trouble and wants to make changes in the performance these must be accommodated as much as possible. Otherwise the performance as a whole will suffer. These changes may include transposing songs on short notice, tuning instruments down, extending a solo, dropping one or two songs or changing the set list so that the comfortable songs are at the beginning and the strenuous ones at the end. On the other hand, the singer has the duty of taking care of his or her voice.

The band or ensemble shouldn't have to compromise because the singer has talked too much, partied too hard or neglected their instrument in any other way.

THE WORK PLACE

Rock, pop and soul singers usually work in the following areas: cover bands, backing vocals, choirs, demo singers for publishing houses/record companies, with their own act, singing waiter/waitress and in certain musicals. Obviously it is important to be multi-facetted if you want to work professionally as a singer. In addition to knowledge, technique and charisma, you need to be able to use your voice as economically as possible as the demands made on it are extreme.

It's not unusual to sing up to twenty songs an evening, four to five days a week. On top of this, the volume on stage is often so high that it is impossible to increase the volume of the singer's monitors without causing feedback. To make up for this one often sings louder than is healthy which leads to voice disorders. This makes awareness of how your voice works and vocal care vital. Below is a fictitious but realistic schedule that will give you an idea of what it takes to live the life of a full time freelance singer. A working week for a fulltime singer may be something like this:

Monday	Backing vocals on CD
Tuesday	Solo performance at local pub
Wednesday	Recording advertising jingles
Thursday	Day off
Friday & Saturday	Apré-ski rock with cover band
Sunday	Day off

MARKETING

Marketing yourself is one of the most important parts of the job. Marketing may include hanging out with like-minded musicians and industry movers and shakers and lobbying. It is also important to main-

Notfabriken

tain contact with colleagues and friends in the business so that they will bear you in mind when a suitable job comes up.

It is important when starting your career or hunting for work that you are aware of exactly what you have to offer. Turning to people who are looking for something else only leads to rejection which in the long run can lower your self esteem. Self esteem is vital.

If you love what you do and what you have to offer it will be contagious, rubbing off on the people you come in contact with and increasing their belief in you. When you consider the various working situations I listed it is obvious that there is potentially an infinite number of demands, relationships and situations to be dealt with.

One thing that is certain however is that to make an impression you will have to stand out from the crowd. Regardless of whether you are dealing with a record company or an audition the most important trait you can have is character! Here are a few things to bear in mind when formulating your marketing plan:

- Only present material that you are satisfied with.
- Don't be afraid to call people you don't know.
- When contacting someone for the first time, rehearse what you want to say and where you want the conversation to lead.
- Don't call at inappropriate times like Friday afternoon or lunch time. This simply creates irritation.
- Never arrive late to a meeting, audition or job.
- Be well prepared.
- Keep a list of people who need to be reminded of your existence. Call them from time to time.
- Try to be seen where the action is. It is important that people are aware that you are in the game.
- Try to remember the names of the people you meet. This instils confidence.
- Be positive, open and believe in yourself. You are unique! There is no one else like you!

LEADING THE BAND

It is important to be familiar with the electronic equipment that is an inevitable part of a rock, pop or soul singer's life as well as the music theory necessary to be able to notate material and instruct your fellow musicians. In addition to music theory this requires a certain knowledge in how other instruments work. Most important of all however is curiosity and the desire to understand how people work in groups. This will help you bring out the best in everyone. What do you do if you join an existing group and have to instruct them in how to perform a song? Here are a few guidelines.

– Choose the key carefully so the musicians don't have to transpose it on the spot. This should only be done in case of emergency when your voice really needs it.
– Provide each member with a copy of the lyrics and music. Include tempo and feel.
– Take a recording of the song with you.
– Play the recorded song and run through the notation. Clear up any questions.
– Always have a metronome at hand so you can set the tempo and count the band in.
– Play the song through once and don't stop even if mistakes are made.
– If you notice that a musician isn't living up to your expectations simplify their part but never show your displeasure.
– After the run through take command by pointing out what has to be done differently: Never say "That was wrong!" Say, "This was more what I had in mind".
– Stay focused and positive. It will rub off.

ELECTRONICS

Avoiding electronic equipment is impossible if you want to be a professional rock, pop or soul singer. Knowing how microphones work is important. You should master certain elements but others require only as passing knowledge. You should have your own microphone, be able to dial in a sound on your sound system, connect a PA, be able to identify

and adjust various vocal elements and be able to convey your requirements to engineers and musicians both live and in the studio.

There are very few bass players that don't have their own bass guitar, very
few guitarists that cannot plug in their instruments and effects, few keyboard players that can't instruct the rest of the band and few drummers
that can't ask for a clearer click track in the studio. So why shouldn't we
know how voice related electronics should be handled?

Microphones

Finding a microphone that captures your voice in the best possible way is
important. Before trying them out though it may be useful to know the
basic principles. There are two main types of vocal microphones for rock,
pop and soul singers:

– Condenser microphones
– Dynamic microphones

A condenser microphone has two thin membranes across which a voltage
is passed. The voltage changes when the membranes vibrate i.e. when
they pick up sound. Condenser microphones produce no power themselves and therefore require an extra power source to charge the membrane. This is known as phantom power and in most cases is available
from mixing boards or separate power supplies that can be connected to
the console.

In dynamic microphones the membrane is attached to a coil of fine wire
placed in the gap of a small magnet. When the microphone pick up a
sound the membrane vibrates which causes the coil to move back and
forth in the magnetic field generating an electric current.

Generally speaking:
Condenser microphones have a broader frequency response which produces a clearer treble and a rapid attack. Their electronics make them sensitive to shocks and moisture. They are ideal in the studio where they do
not have to be moved around too much and where sound quality is especially important for the final recording.

Dynamic microphones have a narrower frequency response but are more robust. They are often unidirectional which stops other instruments leaking in and creating feedback.

Personally, I think it's best to use a good dynamic microphone for rehearsals and live performances and a condenser microphone in the studio or in live situations where the acoustics suit them. In other words I think you should start with a dynamic mike that suits your voice. Find a good music store and try different microphones in your price range. Test them in a PA and compare the following points:

– Which microphone reproduces your sound in the most natural way?
– Which microphone is least prone to feedback?
– How much hand noise do they pick up when you switch hands?

Live microphone technique

Singing with a microphone is natural in rock, pop and soul genres. Microphone technique refers to the technique necessary to make sure the listener experiences as even a volume as possible and also using the microphone as an extra effect when desired. Singers express themselves using different volumes and significant dynamic variations. The microphone passively picks up the sound you present it with so it is up to you to vary the intensity of that sound.

A vocal microphone for live use is unidirectional to avoid sound from other instruments leaking in and increasing the risk of feedback. Therefore it is a good idea to learn to sing directly into the mike and not hold it at your chin. It is common in rock, pop and soul that the volume on stage or at rehearsals is high. This means that you cannot hold the mike too far from your mouth without sound from other instruments leaking in. Another aspect of microphone function is the proximity effect. This is the increase in low frequency energy the closer the microphone is to the source. In other words, the closer to your mouth you hold it the more bass you will get. This can be used as an effect or even the starting point if you like that sound. In certain vocal styles it is customary to have as much bass as possible so singers hold their hand around the microphone cover leaving only a mouth-sized area exposed on the membrane. This means that some of the treble is lost and the sound is perceived as having more bottom end.

You should work out a technique that suits you and note how much you need to move the mike to get the desired effect.

Exercise no. 62 - Live microphone technique

– Hold a dynamic microphone around 1 cm from your mouth.
– Move the microphone to around 5 cm away when you sing loudest.
– Hold the microphone so it lightly touches your lips when you are singing softly or breathily.

Notfabriken

The ideal relative humidity for a singer is 40% or more!

Exercise no. 63 - Studio microphone technique

– Stand 1-30 cm from the puff screen (the net in front of the mike that reduces the "puff" produced by explosive consonants such as [p]).
– Tilt the microphone towards you to avoid unpleasant [s] sounds that can otherwise arise.
– To further reduce "puffs", by forming the consonants at the side of your mouth.

Work towards and away from the puff screen in conjunction with the dynamic changes during the song.

– The studio will naturally have compressor effects to even out the dynamic variations in a song and even a De-esser that eliminates troublesome [s], but it is easier for an engineer to process acoustically well recorded material where effects have been used sparingly.

Notfabriken

Sound systems

Owning your own sound system cannot reasonably be seen as a requirement for the average singer, but being able to handle one definitely is. A sound system consists of a power amplifier, a mixer and speakers.

The amplifier is the part that is responsible for volume. The pre-amp and the amplifier amplify the signals from the microphones and instruments to a level where they can be fed on to the speakers. If you are going to use a condenser microphone you will have to activate the sound system's phantom power. There is usually a button for this.

The mixer will have a number of channels (usually between four and eight on a normal system). There are two different inputs for each channel: Mic and Line. The Mic input is for instruments with low input levels such as vocals, and the line input is for those with stronger input signals such as keyboards. On each channel is a dial that adjusts the input volume: Trim or Gain. This control will boost or lower the signal the instrument produces. Then there are the tone controls which consist of bass, mid-range and treble. This is where you can increase or dial out frequencies to your taste. Finally there is a volume control for your vocals so that they can be balanced against the other instruments.

There may also be an auxiliary control which can be used to send a signal to a reverb unit or stand back monitor.

All of the above controls apply only to the channel in question. Then there is a master section where you will find volume, EQ, effects and inputs/outputs for CD or MP3 players. These controls apply to all of the instruments that are run through the system.

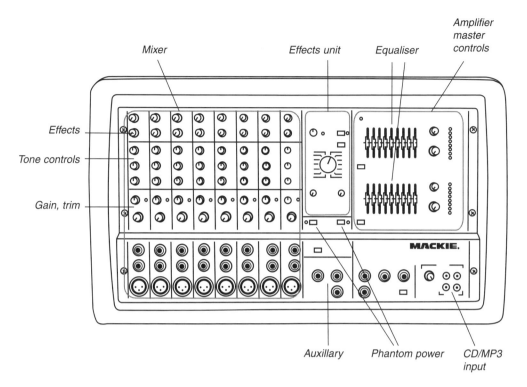

Mixer Effects unit Equaliser Amplifier master controls

Effects

Tone controls

Gain, trim

MACKIE.

Auxillary Phantom power CD/MP3 input

The equaliser is a vital part of the system which enables you to boost or tone down chosen frequencies. They usually have seven or nine frequency bands although there can be as many as 31, ranging from deep bass to high treble. The equaliser gives you the ability to create the basic sound you desire.

The effect unit produces various echo effects such as reverb and delay. Reverb is commonly added to vocals both live and in the studio. Vocals without reverb can sound rough and "dry". Reverb simulates the properties of rooms and surfaces of various types and sizes. For example it can make you sound as though you were singing in a concert hall when you are actually singing in a small room. Delay is also a useful effect for vocals. Delay, or echo as some people prefer to call it, is an effect that slows down part of the sound signal before reintroducing it to produce an echo. You can usually set the delay time and how many times it is to be repeated.

Pre-delay is a function that can be used to set when the effect kicks in. If reverb is making the sound swirl around and the vocals sound muddy, you can use a pre-delay to delay the start of the reverb.

Notfabriken

In this way, the original signal remains dry and crisp while the reverb is rich and full. This helps the vocal bleed into the music.

Cables and contacts are used to connect the instruments to the PA system. Contacts with holes in them are called "female" and those with protruding pins are called "male". The most common types are:

XLR contact:
Male and female are used for connecting microphones.

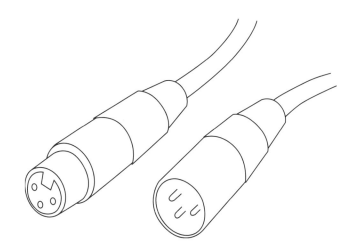

Jack plug:
Used to connect instruments, speakers and external effects.

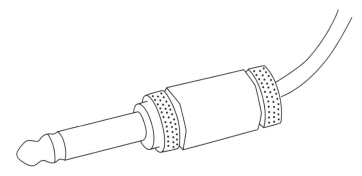

RCA contact and mini-jack

Used to connect equipment such as CD and MP3 players to the mixer board's "tape input".

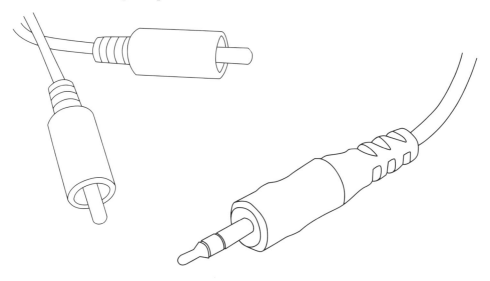

Vocal sound

Learning how to dial in a good vocal sound can take a long time. However, there are a few simple tricks that can speed up the process. Settings are adjusted on the sound system's equaliser, either on that of the microphones channel's or on the master equaliser.

- Vocals produce many overtones in the range 3-5 kHz and will be clearer if you boost these frequencies.
- There isn't much vocal signal to play with under 70 Hz so it can be beneficial to dial out a little of the signal.
- Turn it down before you turn it up. Is the sound muddy? Tone down the bass before you boost the treble.
- Do not dial out too much of the mid-range sound.

THE TEENAGE VOICE

After sports, the most popular activity amongst teenagers is music! Their interest for music, particularly singing is enormous, and the queues for schools of the arts are long. Their interest by no means wanes as they get older and being accepted into college level music studies is difficult due to the limited number of places available. This much we know- singing is popular! We also know that interest is greatest for rock, pop and soul. The problem is that most teenagers admire adult singers in these genres and the songs they attempt to sing are intended for mature voices.

The teenage years are ones of extreme growth, both physically and emotionally. This is perhaps most obvious when teenage boys repeatedly trip over their new, big feet or when their voices "break". These things are a result of rapid growth but also being unfamiliar with their new characteristics. It can take several years before they have mastered their altered bodies. It may even take several years until they settle down emotionally. A boy's larynx will grow dramatically whilst a girl's will grow more moderately. The growth of a boy's larynx means that the thyroid cartilages changes position, the vocal folds increase in size and the fundamental frequency will alter. A boy's voice may drop as much as an octave whereas a girl's will only drop between a third and a fourth. The larynx grows quickly and it will only take between three and six months before they are be able to get to know their "new" voices. A certain amount of growth occurs later in life for both men and women and our ability to control our voices improve with time. In my opinion the best singers are over twenty five, which is no doubt due to a combination of growth and practice which gives greater control of the various components of the voice. The first signs of deterioration appear after the age of 50 when the muscles, tendons and joints become less elastic and the mucosa finds out, all this results in a wider vibrato and a rougher sound.

But let's return to the teenage years where the voice is growing and one has idols who sing material in keys intended for adults with full power in the chest register. This can lead to pushing the voice which can cause injuries that take a long time to heal. It is therefore vital not to press the voice before it has emerged from this period of rapid growth and to watch out for the warning signs of fatigue, namely hoarseness and an aching throat.

THE SPEAKING VOICE

The way we speak often reflects our personality, our emotional state, our social status and origin. The nervous voice is subjected to uneven lung pressure which results in an unstable speaking voice. Men have a tendency to creak while the pitch of some womens speaking voice is too high. Speaking with good vocal technique is one of the most important factors when it comes to preserving our voice. There are many singers who can sing in a technically perfect manner but can't talk more than half an hour without becoming hoarse. For a comprehensive look at the speaking voice I recommend you refer to books devoted to the subject. For the purposes of this book I would simply like to point out the importance of seeing your voice in its entirety. Regardless of whether we sing or speak we are using the same instrument and it is therefore impossible to separate its different uses. I would like to introduce the image of being presented with a bag of voice vibrations every day. We never know how many it is going to contain but the number represents your form on that particular day. The better your daily form, the more you can use it. In the world of rock, pop and soul there are many people who want to be highly visible. This is part of being a performer. This means that singers are often extraverted, active, social people. This type of personality often speaks a lot, fast and at a slightly higher pitch than necessary. Sorting out their speaking voice can make a great difference.

The pitch of the male speaking voice is around "Small" C which is an octave below middle C. A woman's pitch is around a fifth higher than a man's. This differs greatly form person to person and should only be seen as a broad generalisation. Verbal communication in today's society is extremely important and widespread. Voice signatures are used for security systems and internet and video conferences are commonplace. Being able to communicate and still keep your speaking voice in shape is important not only for singers but for everyone. Losing your voice can be a major handicap. Here comes a simple exercise to develop more control of your speaking voice.

Notfabriken

Exercise no. 64 - The Speaking voice

– Breathe in through your nose and relax your shoulders.
– Place a hand on your diaphragm and note that the lower part of your ribcage expands.
– Tighten your stomach muscles as you say: "One!" Dwell on the "n" for a while.

It is important that the tone produced remains voiced and doesn't deteriorate into a creak or "stop". Imagine that you are speaking in a cave where you want the tone to resound and bounce off the walls without straining.

Repeat the above in phrases of various lengths as follows:

Say   1 (one)   1- 2   1-2-3   and so on up to ten.

Remember that each sound should resound, particularly the last one in each phrase.

You would like to remind you that we use the same instrument to sing and to speak, so the breathing exercises and basic exercises from the chapters "Warming up", "Breathing", "Vocal folds" and "Sound" can also contribute to better speaking technique.

One final tip: When speaking in public without a microphone, stand about two meters from the edge of the stage. That way the sound will bounce out to the audience and you won't have to strain your voice.

CHORAL SINGING VERSUS SOLO

Choral singing is an extremely popular past time in many countries. The percentage of rock, pop and soul choirs is open to conjecture, but gospel choirs are becoming increasingly popular and we can definitely put this under the heading "Soul". The technique required for ensemble singing is the same regardless of whether it is in a large choir or backing vocals behind a solo artist. Generally speaking you

Notfabriken

The whitish colour of the vocal folds is due to the fact that very little blood flows through them.

could say that you have to adjust to the collective sound. The goal when singing in groups is usually to create harmonies that result in a certain collective sound and adjusting your sound, vibrato and phrasing to fit in can strain your voice. This is due to the tension that may arise when you are forced to hold back elements of your personal sound or to exaggerate characteristics that feel unnatural to you.

A woman with a thin, alto voice may have to press herself quite hard to produce the full-bodied sound required of gospel altos. One is also limited when backing up other singers.

A backing singer is often chosen because they have certain qualities that enhance the lead artist's performance. (This could be anything from having a voice that complements the star's, the ability to dance, having good ears or even looking good.) If you are lucky your voices will complement each other naturally. If not, you will have to adjust your sound.

It can be difficult to hear yourself in a group. If you can't hear yourself you may be tempted to press your voice which may strain your vocal folds. However, few activities can be as joyful as communal singing.

Singing solo will naturally afford you greater freedom but makes greater demands of your ability to convey emotions and express yourself through your voice. Elements such as improvisation and dynamics are important when singing solo as is the individual quality of your voice. Singing solo is demanding as you are singing constantly without the breaks that singing in groups allows you.

If you are interested in the subject there are many books on the subject of choral singing and many talented teachers that can provide you with more information.

SINGING IN TUNE

Singing in tune is a must for a professional singer. The ability to do so is a result of training and experience. The basis of this ability is the communication between the ear and the larynx which occurs via nervous system impulses to the brain.

The volume of a tone is given in decibels (dB) and the pitch is given in Hertz (Hz)

A sound pressure level of 0 dB is the lower limit for our hearing and 120 dB is the threshold of pain. To put these figures in perspective we can say that an ordinary conversation is around 65 dB and a rock concert around 120 dB. Our ability to discern pitches starts around 20 Hz and sound exceeding 20 000 Hz is inaudible. The range that we hear best is 700-7000 Hz, peaking around 4000 Hz. If you would like more information on how the ear function or hearing impairment you can refer to books on the subject.

We are surrounded by sound in modern society. Even when we think things are quiet there is often a fan in some piece of electronic equipment humming away in the background.

Moments of absolute silence are actually extremely rare. I recommend wearing some soundproof headphones a couple of hours every month just to give your brain and ears a rest. Generally speaking one can say that long term exposure to loud noise or music can damage your hearing and lead to a constant ringing or humming on your ears- a condition known as tinnitus. Tinnitus can significantly reduce one's quality of life so it is important to avoid it at all costs. Hearing impairment amongst singers and musicians is most common in the treble register. Consonants are formed in the treble register which means that one's ability to discern words when doing things like watching TV can be impaired. To avoid this I recommend using some form of hearing protection when singing or playing at high volumes. I also recommend regular hearing tests to discover any hearing loss and prevent it from deteriorating.

A reflex from the ear to the larynx sets the vocal folds vibrating at the frequency the ear picked or picks up. The tone you hear is coloured by:

– The room in which it was produced.
– The vibrations in your upper body.
– The sound that travels directly from your mouth to your ear.

To train our ears and sing in tune we need to:
– Train in the ability to "think" the note before we sing it.
– To tune our voices to a reliable external sound source.

CD
54&55

Exercise no. 65 - Singing in tune

We will train in how to set our voices at a given pitch before actually producing the note. You can do this by singing the major scale below until you know it by heart. Don't sing too loudly as pushing too hard can itself lead to singing off pitch.

– Start by singing the first and second notes and then "think" the other notes when they are played on the piano.
– Then sing the first three notes and "think" the remaining ones.
– Continue in the same way until you can sing all the notes in the scale and still be ready for the coming melody.

As your technique improves you can increase the tempo.

Notfabriken

Exercise no. 66 - Tuning up

This can be compared to a musician tuning his instrument. It is taken for granted that a musician's instrument is in tune when they perform so why shouldn't a singer sing in tune the first time they sing through a song? Here is an exercise for just that. Use a reliable sound source such as a well-tuned piano or preferably an electric keyboard.

Sing "EE" starting on pitch but then gliding under the pianos note until there is a "beating" effect between your note and the pianos. Glide slowly up to the correct pitch so that the beating slows down and finally ceases.

I would like to point out that most people are more tolerant of off key singing if it is sharp rather than flat. In other words how far "off" you can be before it is perceived as off key is greater if you sing sharp, so if you are prone to singing off key it is a good idea to aim a little higher than you think the note is. These exercises will hopefully improve your ability to sing in tune but remember that it takes a long time to acquire "muscle memory", so be patient.

111

THE POWER OF THOUGHT

Mentally preparing yourself for the pitch and sound of a note before you sing it will increase the chances of you producing the desired result as merely thinking about it will trigger nervous impulses that put your laryngeal muscles into the starting blocks. Mental rehearsal is used in many situations. By visualising a successful race athletes can dramatically improve their chances of actually winning. Singers can also use this technique and reap the rewards of positive thinking.

You may have difficulties with certain aspects of your vocal technique when performing in the studio or live. Your mind is a powerful tool and the right attitude and thoughts can be of great help. Here are a few tips for harnessing the power of thought to overcome common vocal obstacles.

Exercise no. 67 - The power of thought

Extended notes

Prepare yourself by inhaling plenty of time before the note: When you start the note focus intensely on the idea that air is coming *in* to your lungs. Start at a comfortable pitch and with narrow vowels such as "EE" and "OO" until you have mastered the thought process and technique.

Low notes

It is also important here to be well prepared as far as breathing and posture is concerned. Do not force the sound. You do not need to sing loudly, just produce a stable tone. Keep you head straight (by thinking "tall"), round your lips, lower your larynx and imagine the note flowing rapidly out of your mouth like a fire hydrant that has burst.

High notes

Imagine that you are sitting on top of the note. Bend your knees a little, focus on tensing the muscles in your neck and the middle of your back and look slightly upwards. Imagine sitting down on the note, as if you were about to sit on something fragile and stopped yourself just in time. Keep "moving" for as long as you hold the note.

These were a few simple visualisations you can use. Your mind is a powerful tool and I'm sure you will be able to put the power of thought and a positive attitude to good use in many challenging situations.

Notfabriken

SUMMARY - A FEW WORDS ABOUT...

- "Fighting the bull" is an expression that reflects the singers leading position on and off stage.
- Rock, pop and soul singers usually work in the following areas: cover bands, backing vocals, choirs, demo singers for publishing houses/record companies, with their own act, singing waiter/waitress and in certain musicals.
- Promoting yourself is one of the most important parts of the job.
- There are two main types of vocal microphones for rock, pop and soul singers: Condenser microphones and Dynamic microphones.
- If you are using an unidirectional microphone the closer to your mouth you hold it the more bass you will get.
- "Turn it down before you turn it up" is a rule of thumb for dialling in a vocal sound.
- Mentally preparing yourself for the pitch and sound of a note before you sing it will increase the chances of you nailing it.
- The size of the vocal folds increase dramatically during puberty thereby lowering the pitch of the voice. A boy's voice may drop as much as an octave whereas a girl's will only drop between a third and a fourth.
- The way we speak reflects our personality, our emotional state, our social status and origin.
- The pitch of the male speaking voice is around "Small" C which is an octave below middle C. The pitch of the female voice is around small G, a fifth higher than men's.
- The ability to sing in tune depends upon the communication between the ear and the larynx which is facilitated via nervous impulses to the brain.
- Hearing impairment amongst singers and musicians is most common in the treble register.
- The sound you hear is coloured by the room in which it was produced, the vibrations in your upper body and the sound that travels directly from your mouth to your ear.
- Most people are more tolerant of off key singing if it is sharp rather than flat in relation to the correct pitch.

XI: Voice care and voice disorders

Voice care is as important to an active singer as it is for an athlete to look after his muscles or a musician to make sure his instrument is in working order.
The best way to care for your voice is to be aware of its limitations, how it works and reacts in different situations and to use this knowledge to plan your singing.

We have previously looked at a singer's working life and have noted that it is common practice to travel to gigs in air-conditioned cars, buses or planes. It is not unusual to be called upon to speak a lot, either during interviews, with promoters or fellow musicians. All this taxes the voice. Developing a voice disorder is quite common and can be due to anything from over exertion to a whiplash injury. Voice function is affected by breathing, digestion, hormones, the nervous system and emotional state of the singer. We will now look at vocal examination techniques and things that positively and negatively affect the voice. We will also consider various voice disorders.

VOCAL EXAMINATION TECHNIQUES

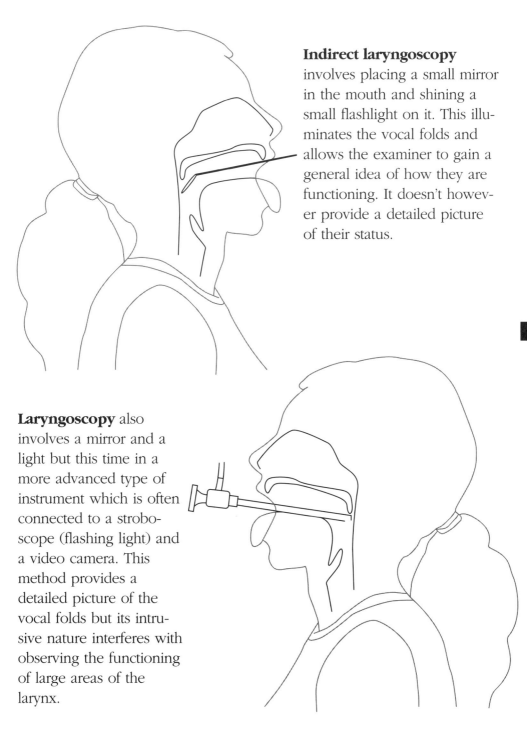

Indirect laryngoscopy
involves placing a small mirror
in the mouth and shining a
small flashlight on it. This illu-
minates the vocal folds and
allows the examiner to gain a
general idea of how they are
functioning. It doesn't however provide a detailed picture
of their status.

Laryngoscopy also
involves a mirror and a
light but this time in a
more advanced type of
instrument which is often
connected to a strobo-
scope (flashing light) and
a video camera. This
method provides a
detailed picture of the
vocal folds but its intru-
sive nature interferes with
observing the functioning
of large areas of the
larynx.

Notfabriken

The vocal folds consist of two mucous membrane folds each containing their own muscle.

Fiber-optic laryngoscopy involves threading a small camera and strobo-scope through the nasal passages and down towards the larynx. In this way the whole larynx can be observed while functioning. The pictures it produces have a lower resolution than those provided by laryngoscopy but the patient can be observed while singing as there is nothing in their mouth to obstruct them.

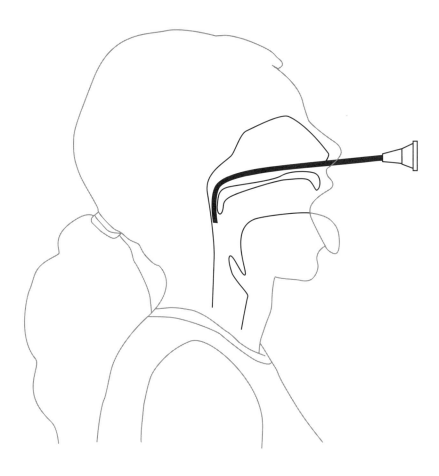

VOICE CARE

These things have a positive effect on the voice:

- Developing your vocal technique to the point where you are able to perform as well as your form on any given day will allow.
- Stretching and getting the blood flowing in your body and vocal tract an hour before you warm up your voice in the morning shower.
- Never singing louder or longer than you voice is prepared for.
- Placing your repertoire in keys that suit you and learning to adjust your sound to the requirements of each individual performance situation.
- Bearing in mind how long you will be singing for each perform-ance. The longer the performance the more important it is not to force your voice in high keys.
- Avoiding going to bed for two hours after a performance so the swelling in your vocal folds can subside.
- Finding your natural range, controlling your breathing when speaking and pausing between phrases.
- Resting your voice (relative rest) for 72 hours after over exertion.
- Using a humidifier in your bedroom or work environment, especially during the winter months if you live in a cold or dry climate.
- Raising the humidity in your hotel room by letting the hot water run in the bathroom while keeping the door open. Particularly helpful during the winter months.
- Making sure you drink approximately one and a half decilitres of fluid per hour evenly distributed over your waking hours.
- Boiling salty water and inhaling the steam after dehydrating trips.
- Breathing through your nose as much as possible when outdoors during the winter.
- Sleeping well. Studies show that our immune systems are sup-pressed by as little as one night's bad sleep.
- Washing your hands often.
- Scheduling interviews *after* gigs.
- Nipping colds in the bud. There is a wide variety of medication to treat the symptoms of colds.

- Preventing dehydration when you have a cold by inhaling steam and drinking lots of fluids.
- Rinsing your nasal passages daily with salt water to prevent colds.
- Maintain your general fitness by exercising regularly and eating healthily.
- Keep your intake of diuretic beverages such as coffee, tea, cola and alcohol to a minimum.
- Treating your coughs with cough medicine.
- Taking care of your respiratory system by avoiding cigarette smoke. Especially important if you are an asthmatic or suffer from allergies.
- Taking your RDA of vitamins and minerals. Vitamins A,E and magnesium are especially important for your mucosa (mucous membranes).
- Eating fruit or chewing sugar-free gum to increase your saliva secretion. Avoid chewing gum for longer than twenty minutes at a time to avoid tense jaw muscles and problems with the your oral mucosa
- Taking a spoonful of olive oil per day. This will raise the amount of fatty acids in your bloodstream and provide your mucosa with a little extra lubrication.

What is best for *your* voice? You may need a long warm up. Singing loudly for long periods may not be a problem for you and you may be able to drink as much coffee as you like. Each voice has its own unique reaction pattern. Knowing exactly how your individual voice works will greatly improve your chances of getting it to work well.

To be kind to your voice, avoid the following:

- Do you clench your jaws or press your tongue against the roof of your mouth while you sleep? This can lead to tension in your jaw and neck which can cause voice problems. If your tongue still has teeth marks along it edges after 12.00 pm it can mean that you are clenching your jaw at night. Just being aware of this can help. In severe cases a mouthpiece may be necessary in which case you can consult your dentist.
- Stress. The stress we are subjected to on a daily basis can have a devastating effect on our voices. Try to find your own personal breathing space. This is well worth it, and not just for your voice.

- Contaminated humidifiers may contain blue algae which can cause asthma so be sure to clean yours regularly.
- If you can avoid it, do not sing when your voice is tired. If you can't avoid it, transpose your songs into a lower key or reduce your patter between songs. Let the backing singers sing as much as possible eg. choruses.
- When it comes to volume, do not sing beyond your technique or louder than is necessary. This is particularly important during sound checks and rehearsals on the same day that you will be performing.
- Rehearsing songs that you do not know well can lead to poor. breath management which in turn can lead to greater strain on your voice. It may be a good idea to take it a bit easy until you know the lyrics and melody.
- Avoid late nights in noisy surroundings, continuously talking loudly and the dehydrating effects of alcohol.
- Lugging heavy equipment has the same effect as weight training and should be avoided just before a gig. Building the high lung pressure needed to lift heavy objects strains the vocal folds.
- Don't sing when you have a cold. Do some light warm ups to keep your voice going but don't exert yourself. Remember that it takes the same amount of time for your mucosa to recover as you were actually sick. In other words, a seven day cold needs seven days of recovery. Do not push your voice during the recovery period. If the cold is mainly a head cold you can try singing a little but be careful! Your sound will be compromised due to your blocked nasal passages and this may tempt you to compensate by pushing too hard. All your mucosa will be inflamed regardless of where you can feel it the most. It can be tempting to sing when a cold is coming on because your voice may actually work really well. Swelling of the mucosa makes it easier to produce a flowing tone, the extra mass giving your voice more body than usual. But do not be deceived! Singing at this stage can aggravate the inflammation.
- Do not run or exert yourself physically outdoors during the winter. The cold air flowing between the vocal folds will dry out the mucosa.
- Avoid hard physical training, both resistance and aerobic, on the same day as a performance.
- Getting the sound in your fold back monitors right is important so

Notfabriken

don't be lazy! You need to be able to hear yourself so you don't have to scream to be heard. If you can't hear yourself boost the frequencies 2-4 kHz. This will bring the vocals out.

- Avoid long conversations on busy streets, in noisy surroundings and on the phone.
- Avoid extreme or habitual throat clearing. Let mucous loosen naturally.
- Do not whistle if your voice is tired. Whistling activates the vocal folds.
- Do not whisper if you are under instructions to rest your voice. It is easy to press your vocal folds when you whisper and the passing air can dry them out.
- Aspirin can have a negative effect on the voice in that its blood-thinning properties may aggravate vocal chord haemorrhages. The effects of the medicine can last for several days. (If you want to be really pedantic, you could say that the same can apply to other painkillers as well. Check with your doctor to see if your medication could increase the time it would take to stop haemorrhaging).
- Do not strain your voice two day prior to, and during your period. At this time your vocal folds will be swollen and the risk of oedema (swelling due to fluid build-up) is increased.
- Do not smoke. Cigarette smoke has a powerful irritant effect on the mucosa and the chemicals it contains can devastate your voice. Smoking can even impair the function of the lower oesophageal sphincter thereby increasing the risk of gastric reflux. (Where stomach acid backs up into the larynx).
- Do not use "smokeless" tobacco. The juice impairs the function of the lower oesophageal sphincter which means that stomach acid can back up into the larynx (reflux).
- Reduce your intake of dairy products when you have a heavy workload as the casein they contain forms thick, sticky mucous.
- Watch your intake of throat lozenges, partly because they can dry out your mucosa but also because they often contain peppermint which can cause reflux.
- Beta blockers, which some artists use to take suppress their anxiety, prevent the heart from beating fast and should be avoided, if not absolutely necessary, if you are going to be doing anything physically active eg. singing and dancing at the same time.

Notfabriken

Asthmatics are usually not permitted to take Beta-blockers as they impair bronchial expansion.
- Avoiding constantly testing your voice the same day as a performance. If you are not in peak form you may become discouraged and the nervous tension this generates will have a negative effect on your voice. Tune in to your form on the day, accept it and work around it. No one is in top form every day.

Remember that everyone is different and some people will have to be more careful with certain things than others. Avoid becoming dependent upon medicine or home remedies to get you through.

Cortisone for Vocalists - The last resort?

I would like to say a few words about cortisone. This is often perceived by professional singers as a wonder drug and abuse is widespread. Cortisone is a drug that is used to suppress the reactions of the body's immune system. The body makes its own cortisone in the form of cortisol – a so-called "stress hormone" that is secreted by the adrenal glands and which plays an important role in our body's defence system. The natural reactions of our immune system in the event of allergies or vocal fold strain result in swelling of the skin or mucosa. Cortisone is used to suppress this reaction. The dose prescribed is often many times higher than the amount produced by the body. If a singer's vocal folds are inflamed due to over-exertion or allergies, cortisone can alleviate the symptoms and allow them to get them through a vital performance such a TV show, opening night or other important showcase. Cortisone is only available on prescription and is usually taken twice on the day of the performance.

Cortisone represses the body's reaction to something it is not happy about. Swelling occurs for a reason. The body is expressing its displeasure with something we have inhaled, eaten or exposed our muscles or mucous membranes to. It is imperative that we listen to our bodies and avoid these situations in the future. If you have a cold, by all means use cold medicine to relieve the symptoms, but do not use cortisone. Cortisone represses the body's immune system and as we will no longer have all our immune resources at our disposal we may actually get worse instead of better. Cortisone shouldn't be used for performances that are *quite* important as this attitude can lead to overuse. The unpleasant side effects of cortisone use are many, not to mention that it may lead to vocal injury. Because the swelling has been medically alleviated, there is a risk that the vocalist will no longer feel when they are over-exerting themselves. This may lead to more serious swelling. Vocalists that take cortisone even though they are healthy and experience that they sing better, may be suffering from mild, chronic inflammation caused by the frequent use of their voice. In this case I recommend that they work on their vocal technique and get to know their limits. In conclusion I would encourage you, whenever possible, to cancel performances when you are sick. Few performances are so important that they will have a long-term effect on your career.

Moreover, the goal is to be able to sing for many years so it is important to cultivate good vocal habits, know your limits and have the foresight to say "no" to gigs that are beyond your capacity or when you are sick or bunt-out. In the event of a major crisis such as a TV performance and where you voice is strained but you are not sick you may turn to cortisone - **as a last resort.**

VOICE DISORDERS

Most professional vocalists will at some time or other, suffer from a voice disorder. This may be caused by anything from a tumour to over-exertion. Underlying causes may be incorrect treatment, skeletal asymmetry, respiratory illness, disease or medication. Your falsetto register may be affected by a night of sleeping with your mouth open and the dehydration this causes, or you may not be able to sing loudly on account of a muscle you strained when whooping with delight.

Notfabriken

The following is by no means a comprehensive presentation of voice disorders, but rather a quick overview to give you some insight into the most common types.

When dealing with voice disorders one usually distinguishes between:
– Functional voice disorders
– Organic voice disorders

Functional disorders are those where vocal impairment is caused by vocal abuse or misuse such as Singing Voice Disorder. Organic disorders involve tissue change, such as nodules.

The distinction between the two categories isn't always clear, but it can nevertheless be helpful to bear them in mind when looking into voice problems.

Vocalists suffering from voice disorders are often prescribed voice rest. There are two types:
– Relative voice rest
– Total voice rest

Relative voice rest means using your voice as little as possible. "Don't say a word you're not getting paid for" as the saying goes. Total voice rest means not whistling or whispering and definitely not speaking or singing. Relative rest is more common and this is usually sufficient to allow vocal injuries to heal. Total rest is an emergency measure taken after vocal surgery or haemorrhages.

The most common functional voice disorders

Phonastenia
Means quite simply, that the voice is worn out through over-exertion or poor technique. The voice is usually ok at the beginning of the day but gets progressively worse as its workload increases. Relative voice rest and training the speaking voice usually leads to improvement.

Singing voice disorder
Hoarseness caused by excessive singing or poor singing technique. Usually treated with relative voice rest and vocal training.

Reflux
Reflux is believed to cause many voice problems. Warning signs include heartburn, waking up hoarse, needing extra-long warm-ups (60 min) and bad breath. Suddenly losing your voice during the day is usually due to reflux. Reflux is where stomach acids back up into the oesophagus, throat and larynx. There are two types of reflux: Gastroesophageal reflux (GERD) is the classic form of reflux that causes heartburn and tightness in the chest. Laryngopharyngeal reflux (LPR) is common amongst singers but is difficult to detect. LPR quickly passes the oesophagus and therefore rarely causes heartburn. Constantly having to clear your throat, a chronic cough and thick mucous can all be signs of LPR. LPR can cause considerable damage to the vocal folds.

124

Treatment can include losing weight, avoiding the following: spicy, fatty, fried and tomato based food, large portions, alcohol (spirits, white wine, red wine, beer in that order), carbonated drinks, caffeine (coffee, tea, cola), lozenges containing peppermint or spearmint, citrus juice and chocolate. One should also avoid eating less than two to three hours before going to bed.

Reflux is most likely to occur during the first hour after a meal, when exerting yourself physically or during the night. Long term use of antacids is common in western society. The injuries caused by reflux can take up to six months to heal. Reflux can persist even if the acidity of the stomach has been reduced which means that just taking medicine alone will not be enough to make a complete recovery. One also has to learn to reduce the effects of stress and adopt a healthier lifestyle.

Puberphonia

Occurs when a boy continues to use his falsetto register because he can't quite find his new bass voice. Treated with speech therapy.

Incomplete glottal closure

Incomplete closure in the middle section of the vocal folds. This is probably due to weakening of the vocalis muscle caused by illness or wear and tear. Thinning of the mucous membranes or scarring on the edges of the vocal folds may also be culprits. The voice sound both "leaky" and strained.

The most common organic voice disorders

Laryngitis (inflammation of the vocal folds)

Acute laryngitis/inflammation of the vocal folds can occur if a singer sings when they have a cold. The vocal folds swell and the voice becomes hoarse. While the infection has been running its course the mucosa have dried out and become red and inflamed. Laryngitis may also be chronic and in this case is usually due to overuse in conjunction with smoking and or alcohol consumption.

Straining your voice when you have laryngitis can result in vocal fold haemorrhaging. Laryngitis increases the risk of dehydrated mucous membranes so it is important that you drink lots of water. Antibiotics are only effective in the event of a bacterial infection. If you absolutely have to perform you may be treated with cortisone and antibiotics. An infection often starts with a virus that subsequently makes conditions more favourable for bacterial growth. Treatment is usually relative voice rest.

Vocal polyps

Polyps are growths on the vocal folds usually caused by vocal abuse in conjunction with a throat infection or previous haemorrhaging. In most cases it is only one vocal fold that is affected (unilateral). Treatment is usually relative voice rest and vocal training, however surgery can be required.

Vocal chord haemorrhaging

If a singer over-exerts themselves when they have laryngitis a blood vessel may burst. If this happens they will hardly be able to make a sound. This is treated with one to six weeks total voice rest.

Vocal nodules

Benign growths on the vocal folds that are usually bilateral (ie. affecting both) and soft or elastic. They arise from vocal abuse in conjunction with upper respiratory infections or colds. They cause hoarseness and difficulty singing softly in the falsetto register. If the nodules are hard they may be surgically removed whereas soft nodules are treated with relative voice rest. However, if they are caused by poor vocal technique they are sure to return. Treatment should therefore include vocal training.

Oedema

Swelling of the vocal folds due to the build-up of fluids. Can arise in conjunction with the hormonal changes caused by menstruation, suddenly shouting or pregnancy. Results in a woolly tone, lowered pitch and difficulty reaching high notes. Can be treated with cortisone and relative voice rest.

Recurrent nerve palsy

The Recurrent laryngeal nerve is the nerve that controls all the internal muscles of the larynx except for the cricothyroid muscles. If this nerve is damaged by a virus or surgery the vocal folds can be paralysed. As long as the paralysis lasts one will be unable to sing. However, function is usually restored after a period of six to twelve months relative voice rest. Persistent paralysis is often treated surgically but in most cases the loss of the singing voice is permanent.

SUMMARY - VOICE CARE AND VOICE DISORDERS

– The three most common examination techniques are indirect laryngoscopy, laryngoscopy and fiber-optic laryngoscopy.

– Voice disorders are extremely common and can range from over-exertion to paralysis.

– Voice function is affected by breathing, the functioning of muscles and mucous membranes, the stomach, hormones, the nervous system and the singer's mental and emotional health.

– Each voice has its own unique reaction pattern. Knowing exactly how your individual voice works will greatly improve your chances of getting it to work well.

– Have the courage to say "no" to gigs when you are sick or bunt-out.

– When talking about voice disorders one usually distinguishes between functional and organic disorders.

– There are two types of voice rest: relative and total.

– Excessive singing when you are hoarse can lead to vocal nodules, polyps, laryngitis and haemorrhaging.

XII: This is your voice

In this chapter we will look at the anatomy and physiology of your voice and teach you how it actually works.

The anatomy of the voice is usually divided into three parts:

– The respiratory system
– The larynx
– The vocal tract

THE RESPIRATORY SYSTEM

The total lung capacity of the adult human male is five to six litres and four to five in the female. Around one and half litres of air remains in the lungs after breathing out. This is known as the Residual lung capacity. The difference between the Total lung capacity and the Residual capacity is known as the Vital capacity and is the air the vocalist has to work with. The air pressure in the lungs is constantly rising and falling in relation to the air pressure around us. To see how it feels when the pressure in your lungs is greater than the external air pressure, say a [p] without releasing any air. To see how it feels when our lung pressure is less than the air around us, exhale as much air as you can and then hold your breath and imagine sucking in air with your mouth closed. The only time our lung pressure is the same as the air around us is at the moment of rest the lungs experience after a deep sigh or a deep breath (known as FRC-Functional Residual Capacity). Phonation threshold pressure (PTP) is the minimum amount of sub-glottal pressure (lung pressure) required to produce the softest of sounds. Singing loudly and at high pitch requires high lung pressure. Singing at a more moderate volume and lower pitch requires less pressure. A popular synonym for lung pressure is "power".

Breathing is what activates your voice. Your respiratory system consists of two complete systems of muscles – one for inhaling and one for exhaling.

Exercise no. 68 Ribcage system

– Place your hands along the lower parts of your ribcage and inhale a small amount of air without expanding your stomach or raising your shoulders.
– Can you feel how the lower part of the ribcage (the floating ribs) expands? The external intercostal muscles spread the ribs to create space for the increased air volume in the lungs.

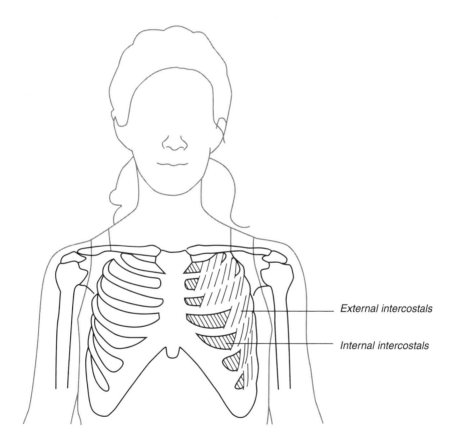

External intercostals

Internal intercostals

When we inhale the external intercostal muscles expand the lower part of the ribcage. When in exhale the internal intercostals contract the ribcage.

Notfabriken

Exercise no. 69 - The Diaphragm system

- Place your hands over your belly button.
- Breathe in through your nose until your lungs are full.
- You stomach will expand because your diaphragm exerts pressure on your stomach pressing your intestines downwards and out.
- When you exhale note **where** the muscles in your body are activated and how it **feels** as they work.

It is the usually the lower stomach muscles (*abdominus rectus*) and side muscles *(internal and external obliques)* that are activated first, followed by the upper stomach muscles and finally - when we are running out of air – the muscles of the lower back (*Quadratus lumborum*).

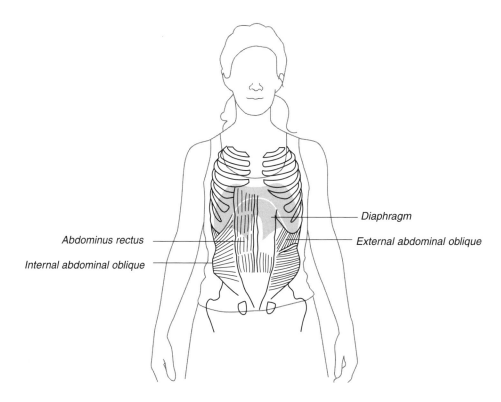

Diaphragm

Abdominus rectus

External abdominal oblique

Internal abdominal oblique

The muscle in this system that controls our inhalation is the diaphragm which is attached to the lower part of the ribcage and the spine. The muscles that control exhalation are the abdominal muscle groups and, to some extent, the lower back muscles.

Notfabriken

Exercise no. 70 - Your "wings"

Many singers believe that the powerful muscles of the upper back can help support their breathing. As far as I know, they have no direct function in our breathing mechanism, but they may direct tension away from the larynx when one sings powerfully. The *latissimus dorsi* muscles are often known as our wings. These are activated when you press your upper arms in against your body, for example when supporting yourself with a microphone stand.

– Squeeze a tennis ball or similar object under each armpit.
– Hold the tennis balls there as you sing a sliding, ascending "hey".
– The further you ascend in your range, the tighter you should squeeze the balls.
– Did you notice that it was easier to keep your larynx relaxed when you activated your back muscles?

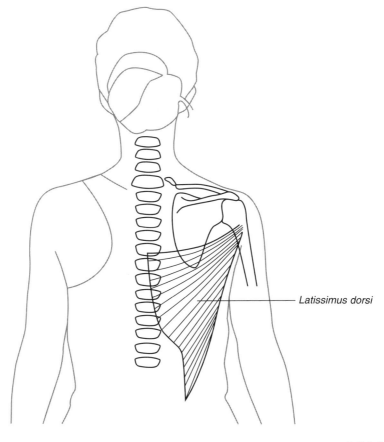

Latissimus dorsi

Notfabriken

THE LARYNX

The larynx produces your voice. It consists of cartilage, muscles and mucosa, all of which are involved in the production of sound. It is located in your trachea (sometimes called windpipe) which is in front of your oesophagus. There are elongated cavities called *sinus piriformes* located just behind and to the sides of the larynx.

Without going into too much detail, starting at the bottom of the larynx is the Cricoid cartilage. Attached to it are the Thyroid and Arytenoid cartilages. The front part of the vocal folds is attached to the front edge of the thyroid cartilage and at the back they are each attached to their own arytenoid cartilage. On the top and bottom of the thyroid cartilage are small "horns". The upper horns are attached to the hyoid bone and the lower ones to the cricoid cartilage. Above the vocal folds are the Vestibular folds, also known as the "False vocal folds". These are used in certain types of forceful singing. Lastly we have the Epiglottis that forms a seal when we swallow preventing food from entering the lungs. The larynx can be raised and lowered and its position will affect the colour of the sound.

Exercise no. 71 - Larynx height

- Place your thumb and forefinger on your Adam's apple.
- Yawn and note how your larynx moves down.
- Keep your fingers on your larynx.
- Swallow! Did you feel how your larynx moved up?

The distance between the uppermost and lowest larynx positions is around five centimetres and makes a great difference both to your sound and the strain placed on your voice. If you want to be able to take vocal instructions you will need to master these two movements.

Volume doubles for every third dB.

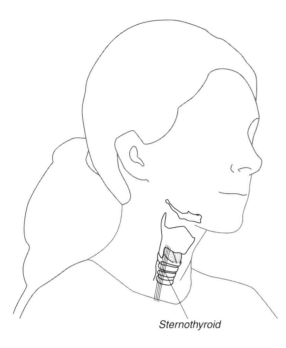

Sternothyroid

The downward movement of the larynx is caused by the *Sternothyroid muscles* in conjunction with other muscles and around six different pairs of muscles are involved in upwards movement of the larynx. Generally speaking, muscles that attached to the Thyroid cartilage and below pull the larynx down, whereas muscles that are attached to the Thyroid cartilage upwards pull the larynx up. These muscles are called the *External laryngeal muscles.*

Exercise no. 72- Cartilage tilt

– Find the little indentation a few centimetres under the Adam's apple.
– Place your forefinger just over it and your middle finger just under it.
– "Squeal like a pig", softly and slightly distorted.
– Did you feel how the cricoid cartilage disappeared inwards? (Or did the thyroid cartilage move out?)
– Now you know how it feels when the thyroid and cricoid cartilages is tilted.

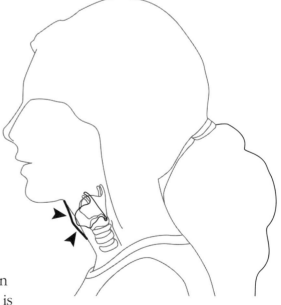

The length of the vocal folds can be divided into two parts:
– Cartilaginous
– Membranous

Exercise no. 73 –
Your vocal fold openers

– Breathe in!
The muscles that opened your vocal folds to
allow air in were your *Posterior cricoarytenoid
(POST) muscles.*

Posterior cricoarytenoid

Exercise no. 74 - Your vocal fold closers

– Softly and breathily sing a note at a comfortable pitch.

Now the Interarytenoid (IA) muscles have pressed the back part of the
Arytenoid cartilages. The Lateral Cricoarytenoid (LCA) muscles have
pressed the vocal folds together by pulling the Arytenoid cartilage forwards. This causes them to rotate, bringing together the vocalis process.
The leakage that occurs is probably due to the fact that neither the cartilaginous part, the rear third of the vocal folds or the membranous part
(the front 2/3 of the vocal folds) are fully pressed together.

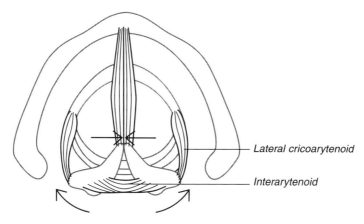

Lateral cricoarytenoid

Interarytenoid

Notfabriken

Exercise no. 75 - Your gear stick

– Sing a loud "Ahoy!"

Now the vocal folds have come together along their entire length, the entire vocal fold mass is oscillating and the vocalis muscles are contracted.

If you imitate the voice of a young child and say "I don't want to go to school today!" you will probably be using your falsetto register. In this register your vocalis muscles are most likely not contracted and only the outer part of the vocal folds are oscillating. The leakage that occurs in the falsetto register is from both the cartilaginous and membranous parts.

The inner parts of the vocal folds (*Thyroarythenoid-TA*) are known as the *vocalis*. The vocalis makes the vocal folds shorter and thicker. The vocalis is one of the toughest muscles in the body and can remain contracted even when highly stretched, as happens when we sing at high pitches with closed vocal folds, in our chest register.

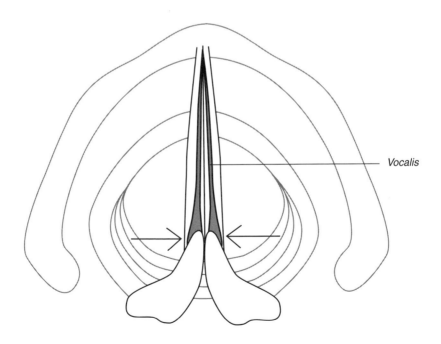

Vocalis

Exercise no. 76 – Your vocal fold stretchers

Place a finger on your larynx, just under the upper edge of the Adam's apple (about 1 cm for women and 2 cm for men). You will feel a small opening which is the gap between the cricoid and thyroid cartilages.

Softly sing a comfortable note and then glide upwards, continually raising the pitch. Feel how the opening closes. It may be a little difficult to feel this, especially for women because their larynx is smaller.

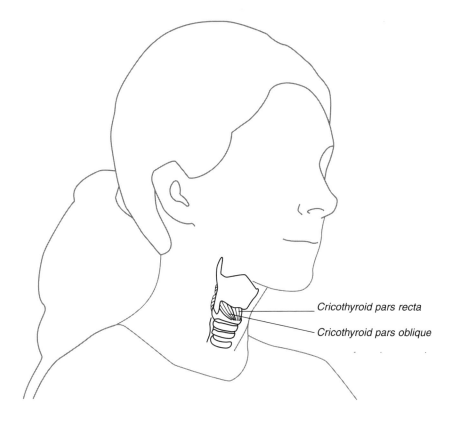

Cricothyroid pars recta

Cricothyroid pars oblique

To raise the pitch of the note we need to increase the frequency of the vocal fold oscillations. This is done by increasing air pressure and stretching the vocal folds. The thyroid and cricoid cartilage muscles (*Cricthyroid pars recta* and *Cricothyroid pars oblique)* are responsible for this. These muscles are located between the cricoid and thyroid cartilages.

Notfabriken

Exercise no 77 - Vocal fold mucosa

Softly sing a note at comfortable pitch! The mucous membranes of the vocal folds are probably the only things vibrating right now.

The vocal fold mucosa are extremely important. Their condition will immediately be reflected in your singing. We will now take a closer look at its parts:

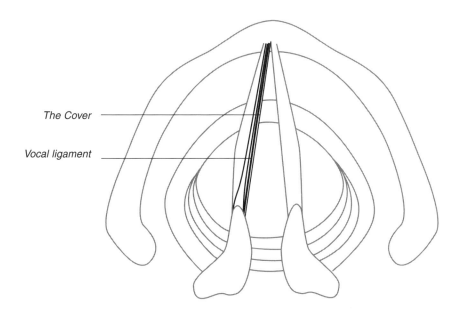

The Cover

Vocal ligament

The mucosa is approximately 1 mm thick and consists of four layers and two sections:

The cover: Consists of the *epithelium* (which has the same consistency as your skin) and the outer layers of the *lamina propria* (which has consistency of a thick liquid)

The vocalis ligament: Consists of the middle and deep layers of the *lamina propria* (which has the consistency of a thin fascia)

Notfabriken

Exercise no. 78 - Your "false vocal folds"

– Loudly clear your throat or roar like a lion!

Now the *vestibular folds* are brought together (adducted). Imagine that you are a "lady of breeding" receiving guests and smile with your eyes and face. Your vestibular folds have now most likely moved apart (abducted).

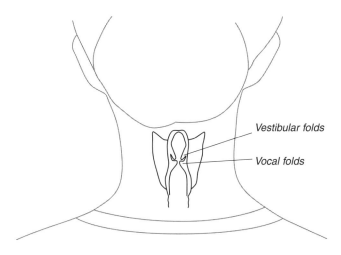

Vestibular folds

Vocal folds

Exercise no. 79 - Your "twanger"

– Imagine that you are teasing someone and sing "Na, na, na, na, na, na".

The little muscle that sits around the larynx like a collar is known as the "twang muscle" (*Aryepiglottic sphincter*). When this muscle contracts, the upper part of the larynx narrows and the sound produced becomes shriller. As yet this is only a theory as the scientif- ic evidence is not conclusive.

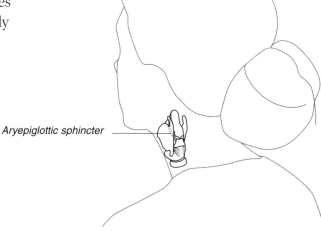

Aryepiglottic sphincter

Exercise no. 80 – Your Epiglottis

– Swallow!

The epiglottis will now form a lid over the larynx, closing it off. This action prevents food and drink from entering the lungs.

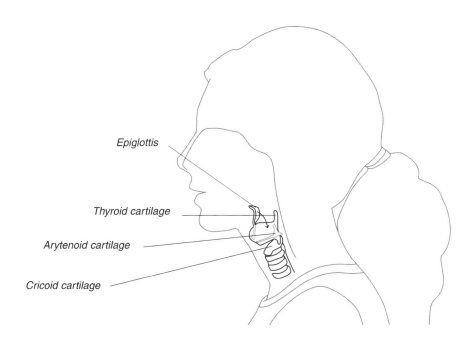

Epiglottis

Thyroid cartilage

Arytenoid cartilage

Cricoid cartilage

We can conclude this section by pointing out that all the muscles and cartilages that we have mentioned, plus many more, determine the force, breathiness and pitch of the note before it is sent on to your resonator- the vocal tract.

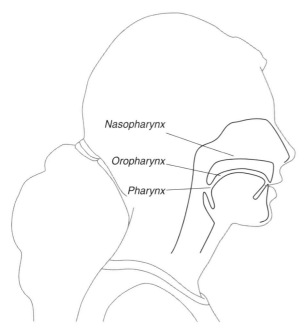

Nasopharynx

Oropharynx

Pharynx

Exercise no. 81
- Your vocal tract

Your vocal tract are your voice's resonators. This is where the sounds of speech are formed.
– Sing a loud "oh hey!" The shape of your vocal tract changed while singing.

The vocal tract are the spaces between the vocal folds and the lips. It is approximately 15-25 cm long and consists of the throat, oral cavity (mouth) and nasal cavity

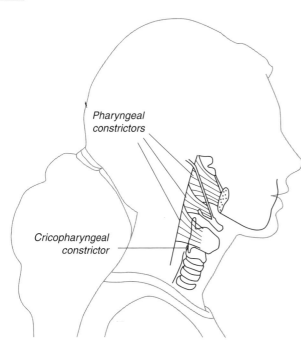

Pharyngeal constrictors

Cricopharyngeal constrictor

Exercise no. 82 –
Your swallowing muscles

Relaxing or tensing the constrictor muscles in your throat can affect the production of overtones and thereby your sound.
– Say a drawn-out whiny "NO!!", while descending in pitch. (Like a disappointed teenager). Note how your throat tenses.
– Say a surprised, ascending "WHAT??!" Your swallowing muscles will most likely be relaxed.

Here are the muscles that affect the way your throat colours your sound:

Notfabriken

Exercise no. 83 – Nasality

The nasality of a note is determined by the amount of the note passing through the nasal cavity.

- Say: "Song!" Note how the back of the tongue touches the soft palate.
- Stay with the "ng" sound and sing a note.
- Hold your nose! Did you notice how your ears felt blocked and how it affected your sound?
- Hold your nose and exhale with a "gah!" sound. Note that all the sound comes out through your mouth.
- Switch between "ng" and "gah" to train the muscles that control the soft palate.

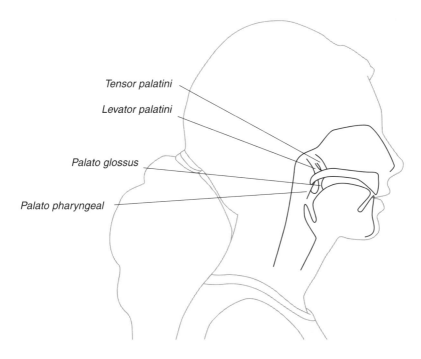

Tensor palatini

Levator palatini

Palato glossus

Palato pharyngeal

The *levator* and *tensor palatini* close your nasal cavity while the *palato glossus* and *palato pharyngeal* open it.

The tongue also plays an important role in the formation of your sound. Changing the shape of the tip or the back alters the space in the vocal tracts and also the sound produced. The tongue can be changed in all directions and is involved in many aspects of vocal technique. The tongue can also suffer from tension that negatively affects the voice. The tongue is a complex muscle and a detailed description of its anatomy and function is beyond the scope of this book.

This has been a description of the fundamental parts of our vocal system. It should be noted that there are many other important connections between muscles and ligaments as well as a plethora of anatomical components that have not been mentioned here but affect the voice.

SUMMARY - THIS IS YOUR VOICE

– The anatomy of the vocal system is divided into three parts: the respiratory system, the larynx, and the vocal tract.

– Your respiratory system consists of two complete systems.

– A distinction is drawn between active and passive breathing.

– The vocal folds are located in the larynx, and just above them are the vestibular folds.

– The larynx determines the pitch of a note and the register used.

– The *vocalis* is the middle part of the vocal fold muscle.

– The vocal fold mucosa is approximately 1mm thick and is consists of four layers and two sections: the cover and the vocalis ligament.

– The vocal tract are the areas between the vocal folds and the lips and consist of the throat, the oral cavity (mouth) and the nasal cavity.

FAQ

- I am an 18 year old guy that sings a lot. I would like to improve my voice but most of all I would like a husky voice. Is it possible to develop a husky voice by singing a lot?

- A horse voice can be produced by congenital or acquired asymmetry in the vocal mechanism. Singing yourself horse is not a good idea as it can lead to you not being able to sing at all. Instead, you should learn how to sing with a breathy quality although this is nothing you should attempt on your own. Consult a singing teacher.

- Hi! I have been singing and performing for most of my life. Two years ago I was on tour for nearly a year and started to drink, smoke and party. I noticed that my voice became rougher and "drier". Sometimes I have difficulty hitting high notes in the chest register.

- It is tempting to start partying and smoking when on tour and this more often than not results in your voice taking a beating. You should consult a singing teacher who is used to working with this problem and learn a new technique that works for you. It may be an idea to learn more about voice care and to have a medical examination to determine if your voice has sustained any physical injuries.

- Have always wondered how some singers can riff and slide effortlessly between notes.

- The reason some singers can do this is that they have trained a lot. Of course genetics play an important role as well. Softer voices ie. voices with shorter vocal folds and less vocal fold mass, have an easier time quickly changing pitch than more powerful voices.

- *Why do some people have better singing voices than others despite having undergone the same amount of training?*

- The question is really, what is meant by singing "well"? It may be said though that certain singers have superior technique and have mastered the various dimensions of the voice. This means that they can sing in tune, softly, powerfully, high and low and can express themselves as they like through their voice. The fact that some are better than others despite equal amounts of experience is quite simply a matter of talent. Vocal talent is not just a question of being able to produce the notes but also the ability to master musical nuances and present an appealing sound.

- *I love singing and have devoted my life to it. I wonder how I can make industry contacts and maybe record a demo.*

- I think you should start buy enrolling in a singing course where there will be like-minded people. If you already have a demo, send it to various music publishing houses and see if they would like to hire you as a demo singer.

- *Hi there! If you have sung at a very high standard for many years and then had a break for a few years, will your voice quality have deteriorated? Does the voice continue to get worse after thirty? How long is it in its prime? At what age are you "finished" as a singer?*

- Hard to know exactly what you mean by "high standard". Do you mean that you worked as a singer or that you had a voice as good as a professional singer? The voice works just like the rest of the body. If you don't train, your fitness deteriorates. On the other hand, as is the case with all activity, if you have previously trained hard at something it will be relatively easy for you to pick it up again. In my opinion the best singers are between 25 and 50 years old. A voice isn't "old" until close to 60.

- How many hours a day can you practice without damaging your voice?

- Generally speaking it is hard to say how long you can practice each day. As long as your technique is good and you feel fresh at the start of each day, you obviously aren't doing anything wrong. The stamina of your muscles depends on oxygen supply and uptake and is highly individual. I will go out on a limb however and say two hours a day including warm up and cool down.

- I am a 15 year old girl who loves to sing, but sometimes I feel I strain my vocal folds because I get a really sore throat. Why is this so and what can I do about it?

- The reason your throat hurts may be because you are straining your vocal folds beyond their limits by singing too high or too loud. It could be that your voice is breaking (yes, this happens to girls too!) which is a tricky period for the voice but fortunately is only temporary. You're probably also singing songs that are written for adult performers and that are too high for you. A rule of thumb: If you get a ticklish cough or a sore throat, rest your voice! You should also take lessons to improve your technique and vocal awareness.

- I have always wanted to sing. My greatest dream is to be a singer, but my voice won't cooperate. Seriously, I sound pretty bad! I don't know what to do. Is there anything I can do to learn to sing or must I start from the beginning? It really is my ultimate dream.

- First of all, to be a good singer you must like singing. Don't compare yourself to others and try to let go of preconceived notions of how you "should" sound. Taking lessons or buying an instructional book is a good place to start. Sing often and joyfully and you will eventually come to like your voice and even sound good to others. Unfortunately there are no shortcuts to becoming a great singer.

- I have sung in bands for 10 years (I am 26). For most of this time I have had a clear falsetto, but about a year and a half ago it just disappeared and I can't even remember under what circumstances. When I try to sing a little tentative falsetto it sounds hoarse and a hissing sound is produced as the air is pressed out. At higher pitches and with greater air pressure I can sing falsetto. My chest register is fine, it's just the falsetto that's affected. I have been to a doctor and he examined me with a camera and said that my vocal folds were healthy.

- Singing falsetto is technically difficult. The falsetto register is often associated with a breathier quality which is due to the fact that the vocal folds are not fully closed. If the vocal folds are a bit swollen or irritated the falsetto register will be the first to be affected. This is because only the edges of the vocal folds vibrate when singing falsetto and if the mucosa is irritated it can be harder to get them vibrating properly. The instruments used for medical examinations aren't fine tuned enough to see the differences we can feel. I suggest you start by working gently with your voice together with a singin teacher. Singing forcefully is not to be recommended before you have remedied the situation.

- Hi. I'm an 18 year old guy who's into hard rock. Our style of music is based on an aggressive singing style we call "growling". It may just sound like screaming, which it is actually, but if you just scream you can't growl for more than one song before your voice is shot. I've heard that you should growl from your stomach but I'm not sure what to do.

- Generally speaking, when you growl you are constricting a large portion of the larynx and the vibration that ordinarily just involves the vocal folds is extended to include the supraglottal mucosa. Growling is extreme singing and requires a tough and resilient voice. Singing from your stomach, which is also known as support, is controlling your breathing using your abdominal and intercostal muscles. Support relieves the strain on your vocal folds and can really be needed when growling. Even so, growling is extremely strenuous and even the perfect breathing strategy can't compensate for the wear and tear it causes. Another factor is that certain singer's voices can take more punishment than others. Some singers also have more flexible supraglottal structures than others.

- *Hi there! I am a happy-go-lucky girl who loves to sing. When I grow up I would like to sing. The problem is that I can't sing in high keys. What should I do? I would also really like to be a singing teacher and would be grateful for any tips.*

- You don't say how old you are. The voice is continually developing and doesn't peak until around 25 - 40 years of age. Learning to sing in high keys is best done with the help of a vocal trainer. But singing high notes shouldn't be an end in it self. It is important that you cultivate your own individual voice according to your ability and limitations. All well-known singers have a special quality to their voice and this is more important than being able to reach high notes. However, I understand your frustration and the chances of being able to expand your range are good. Sing often and try to keep your voice in good shape and you are sure to improve. If you want to be a singing teacher you will have to practice singing, study music theory, learn a little about other instruments and eventually apply to a college of music or conservatory.

- *Some singing teachers claim that one's range can only be extended a few tones, while others say that it possible to gradually draw the vocal folds together from one end to the other like a zipper and in this way reach very high notes. Could you explain this as I am very curious? Thanks.*

- When talking about extending your range a tone or two, we usually mean vocal fold adduction (closing) along their entire length, with the possible exception of the vertical mass. As pitch increases the vertical mass becomes thinner, and when the register shift between chest and falsetto registers occurs, the vocal folds are stretched very thin and only their edges are vibrating. There is usually a gap in the adduction when singing falsetto so you could say that you are only singing with part of the vocal folds. In other words it is not possible to close the vocal folds like a zipper although once in motion the vibrations can take any form.

- Why do some singers' voices tire quickly while others can sing forever?

- It may depend on technique, wise choice of keys and genetic factors – some people's mucosa, tendons and muscles can simply take more punishment than others. The percentage of red and white muscle fibres also plays a part. White muscle fibres are able to eliminate lactic acid and are therefore long distance muscles whereas red muscle fibres are sprinters. If you train at singing for long periods you will probably be able to shift the balance a little and therefore improve your stamina but bear in mind that we all have different tolerances.

- I have been having problems with clogged sinuses for years. It feels like there is some sort of resistance in my forehead when I sing- it doesn't feel clear. At rehearsals I am often encouraged to "send the note out to my head" to improve the resonance, but it feels like something is blocked in my forehead. When I do resonance exercises like [m] and [n] it feels like I can't find any space to use.

- The sinuses contribute to overall resonance but they only play a minor roll. The vocal tract (throat, mouth and nasal cavity) is the most important factor. If you direct your sound towards your nasal cavity and sinuses and they are blocked it will feel like running into a wall. However, because the majority of your resonance comes form your vocal tract it is still possible to produce a resonant sound even if the resonant properties of your sinuses are impaired It is probably more appropriate for you to concentrate your efforts on your clear areas such as your mouth and perhaps your nose and not on the blocked areas such as your sinuses.

- Do you need as much support for soft notes as loud ones?

- The purpose of support is to supply the optimal lung pressure to produce the desired pitch and volume. A high note in the chest register usually requires greater lung pressure ie. the louder and higher a note (volume usually follows pitch) the greater the lung pressure – support. So the answer is no! The strength of your support should naturally follow the volume of the note and therefore should not be as powerful when singing softly.

Notfabriken

- *Hi! Can you suggest an image or visualisation I can use when I stand on stage and have to "give it all I've got"*

- I believe that it all comes down to will, desire and conviction. Singers with a strong faith such as Christian singers, often have an easier time "giving it all". Imagining that you are singing for one special person in the audience or concentrating on giving them the best experience possible may help. It may also be a question of pure will power – for example having a clear mental picture of what you want to achieve at an audition. Generally speaking it usually helps to make a conscious decision prior to the gig to give it your all and to know why you're giving it.

- *My previous singing teacher insisted that removing your tonsils could have a positive effect on your voice as it frees up the working area of the larynx and muscles by removing obstructions.*

- Removing your tonsils may make you less prone to throat infections and may affect your sound in that the anatomy of your vocal tract has been changed. However, it will have absolutely no effect on the way your larynx works as the tonsils are not in its way!

- *Hi! I have recently developed a very disturbing problem. I feel that my voice has become "wobbly" and unstable. All of a sudden I can't sing without producing an irritating vibrato. It depends a little on my daily form. I sing quite a lot and have done so for the past 15 years, often in short, intensive periods followed by a break of a month or two. Suspect that this pattern is not ideal. Could I have an injury or is it my age (30)? Hope I'm just out of shape and that training will make it go away.*

- It is definitely not because of your age, but rather because you sing sporadically. A "wobbly" vibrato is largely due to poor breathing control. This can be because you are vocally out of shape and don't have the fitness required to manage your breathing and stabilise your larynx. Practice a little every day so you don't "lose ground" during your breaks.

- Hi! Tom Jones is a singer that sings in rather high keys and, almost always, very powerfully. To me it sounds as though he sings with a low larynx position, at least compared to most others singers in this genre. His sound at high pitches is reminiscent of classical singing. It sounds like certain frequencies are amplified in a way that would not be possible with a higher larynx position. This must be because the resonance tract are affected. My experience is that in certain cases tone is strengthened and has more punch when the larynx is low. Is this the case? Drawing the comparison with classical singers once again, they can be heard over the orchestra even though they don't strain that hard, because they have sound quality that is more penetrating than a pop singer's. My question is then, if two notes are produced with the same amount of force, would one produced with a low larynx be louder in dB than one produced with a high larynx?

- You are referring to an amplification of frequencies known as a singer's formant! This is created when the frequencies of formants 3, 4 and 5 approach each other. When this happens they create one large overtone peak instead of three smaller peaks. To achieve this it is probably necessary to lower your larynx in the manner of a classical singer. The sound that is produced is one that we usually associate with opera. Singing with this type of sound in the rock, pop and soul genres would probably not go down too well. I would imagine that Tom Jones has a large vocal tract but his singing does not involve a singer's formant. The volume (dB) and subglottal pressure a singer can produce is highly individual so it is difficult to generalise when comparing vocalists' volume. However, we can say that when a formant is formed the perceived level increases although acoustically speaking the level remains unchanged. I would conclude therefore that the listener will perceive vocals as louder when the singer sings with a singer's formant even though they are singing with the same subglottal pressure. Remember however, that there are many technical aspects that must be considered if you want to sing powerfully and maintain good vocal health.

Musical and vocal glossary

This glossary is a mixture of slang terms used in the music industry, general musical terms and anatomical and physiological terms pertaining to the voice. The explanations provided are simplified so please refer to other reference books for more comprehensive definitions.

Abduction	Moving the vocal folds away from each other (opening)
A cappella	Singing without musical accompaniment
Accelerando	Continually faster tempo
Accent	Stress or emphasis of a note through amplification or pro-longation
Adagio	Slow tempo
Adduction	Moving the vocal folds towards each other (closing)
Ad lib	Improvising as you like.
Aphonia	Inability to phonate (speak)
Airplay	Getting songs played on radio and TV
Acoustic	Without amplification
Al coda	Go to the "coda" (last part of a song) Coda = tail
Al fine	Go to the "Fine" symbol (end of a song)
Alla breve	2/2 or "cut time"
Allegro	Quick tempo
Alto	Voice category in classical singing with a range of approx f to f2
Amplifier	Unit for increasing the level of sound signals
Analog	Direct recording of sound to a magnetic tape. Compare with digital.
Arrangement	The way the various instruments played in a piece of music are organised

Notfabriken

Arpeggio	The notes of a chord played one after the other
Articulation	Shaping the sounds of speech and singing
Arytenoid cartilage	Is connected to the rear part of the vocal folds and contributes to abduction and adduction.
A vista	Sight reading. Singing from a musical score without having seen it before.
Backdrop	The background on stage, usually made of cloth or paper and containing the artist's or band's name or logo.
Backline	The amplifiers that musicians typically have behind them on stage to amplify the sound of their instruments
Backstage	The area behind the stage
Backing track	CD or other media with pre-recorded accompaniment.
Baritone	Voice category in classical singing with a range of approximately G to g1.
Bass	Voice category in classical singing with a range of approximately E to e1
Bass clef	Clef that defines the second line down in music notation as small f and which is used to notate music in the lower registers (the bottom half of the piano keyboard)
Beat	Term for the rhythmic component of a piece of music
Belting	Powerful singing at high pitches in the chest register.
Bpm	Beats per minute. The tempo of a piece of music.
Bridge	Passage in a song that often differs melodically from the rest of the song.
Bullet	Term used for a song that climbs rapidly up the sales charts
Call & response	A singer or musician sings or plays a phrase to which another musician responds musically.
Casting	Assigning rolls in a show

Cesur	Symbol indicating a pause for breathing
Chops	Riffs. The ability to play a musical instruments
Chord	Three or more notes played together
Chord chart	Simplified notation showing chord progressions
Chorus*	The part of a song that is repeated at intervals.
Chorus**	A sound processing effect that produces a fuller sound.
Circle of fifths	A circle depicting the relationship between the twelve keys in steps of a fifth
Climb	Also known as pre-chorus. A two or four line section immediately preceding the chorus.
Coaching	Expert help
Chromatic	Motion in half tone steps
Closing phase	Phase of vocal fold oscillation where the folds are closed.
Combo	Combined amplifier and speaker
Compressor	Effect that evens outs dynamic variations
Consonant	A speech sound produced by partial or complete obstruction of the airflow
Covering	Changing the position of the vocal tract and vocal folds to produce a deeper sound quality. Used to relieve static larynx height.
Crescendo	A gradual increase in volume or intensity
Crew	The people who work with light and sound at concerts
Cricoarytenoid muscles	Join the arytenoid and cricoid cartilages that are responsible for abduction and adduction of the vocal folds.
Cricothyroid muscles	Elongate the vocal folds to raise pitch
Cue	A signal to begin or change parts of a song
Da Capo (D.C.)	Indicates that the song is to be played once again from the beginning

153

Dal segno (D.S.)	Play or sing from the Segno symbol in the notation.
Decay	The receding of a note.
Decibel (dB)	The unit of measurement of sound level (volume)
Demo	A recording of songs for promotion purposes
Diaphragm	Large muscle in the torso that is responsible for inhalation.
Didactics	The theory of teaching
Diphthongs	A monosyllabic vowel combination involving a quick change from one vowel sound to another without an interceding consonant
Digital	Where sound is sampled in binary form/data pulses.
Diminuendo	Gradual decrease in volume or intensity
Diplophonia	A condition where two notes are phonated simultaneously
Dissonance	An harmonically unpleasant combination of notes
Distortion	Sound that is overdriven
Doubling	Using the same recording on two separate tracks. Often used to give vocals a fuller sound
Dry run	Rehearsing without instruments
Dynamics	Variations in volume and intensity
Effect	Electronic means of altering the character of the original sound
Ensemble	A group of musicians or actors who perform together.
Epiglottis	Structure at the root of the tongue that closes off the trachea when swallowing to prevent food and drink from entering the lungs
Equalising	Evening out varying voice qualities between vowels and registers.

Notfabriken

Equaliser	Tone control device used to enhance or diminish different frequency bands.
Falsetto register	Voice register above the chest register, characterised by large, round vocal pulses, a strong root note, short closed phase and incomplete adduction.
False vocal folds	The Vestibular folds which are located above the Vocal folds (true vocal folds)
Feedback	Sound produced when a microphone is held too close to its speaker regenerating the sound and producing a howling sound.
Female contact	Electrical contact with recessed holes
Final rehearsal	Rehearsal using the exact same equipment and format as the final production
Flageolets	Overtone produced on a stringed instrument
Flight case	Hard instrument case designed to withstand the rigours of travelling
Flow phonation	Phonation with moderate subglottal pressure, generous air flow and the least possible vocal fold activity required to achieve adduction.
Follow spot	A narrow spotlight, used to 'follow' or to spotlight a performer on a stage
Formant	Resonance in the vocal tract. There are five important formants.
Forte	Powerfully
Frequency	The number of oscillations per seconds. The greater the number, the higher the perceived pitch.
Fry	Vocal register characterised by a very low pulse frequency. Produces a "creaky" sound similar to bacon frying.
Ghost note	A soft percussive stroke or note performed in between standard notes
Gig	A paid job. Originally a musicians' term but now used more widely.

Gimmick	Promotional strategy highlighting a particular characteristic of a performer
Glissando	Sliding between a series of consecutive notes
Glottal wave	The wave-like movement of the vocal fold mucosa during phonation
Groove	The overall rhythmic character of a piece of music
Harmony	The study of chord structure
Headliners	The main act at a concert
Hook	The part of the song that sticks in your memory.
House lights	General purpose lighting in a venue. ie the lights that are on before the concert when people are finding their seats
Hype	Excessive publicity or exaggerated claims
Hyperphonation	Phonation with excessive muscular activity
Hypophonation	Phonation with insufficient muscular activity
Hz	Hertz. Unit used to measure frequency.
Improvisation	Spontaneous composition
Instrumental	Music without vocals
Intercostal muscles	Muscles between the rib bones that are used for breathing
Interval	Difference in Hz between two notes. i.e. the distance between two notes in a scale.
Intonation	Finding the right frequency so that a note sounds "in tune".
Intro	Introduction. The first part of a song or show.
Jam session	Informal gathering of musicians to improvise or play unrehearsed music.
Jingle	Short musical piece used in a commercial or promo spot.

Larynx	Primary organ of voice production. Consisting of a moveable cartilage structure.
Larynx tube	The short tube shaped cavity between the trachea and the throat.
Lead sheet	A form of condensed musical notation making it easier to sight read. Includes tempo, chords, lyrics and melody.
Legato	Literally "tied together" Notes are played smoothly without any intervening silences. Opposite of staccato.
Limiter	An effect that clips signals that exceed a pre-set limit
Line box	A box that leads cables from an instrument to the PA
Line check	Checking the signal strength and balance between an instrument on stage and the mix sent to the fold back monitors and PA.
Loop	A recorded figure that is constantly repeated
LTAS	Long Term Average Spectra. Shows the average sound level across different frequency bands.
Major	Scale or chord characterised by a major third above the root
Male contact	Electrical connector with exposed prongs
Merchandise	T-shirts, posters, accessories etc sold on tour
Methodology	Teaching methods
Metronome	Device for keeping time
Miking up	Setting up microphones in front of a sound source to amplify the sound and send it to the PA
Minor	Scale or a chord characterised by a flattened third above the root note.
Modal register	See Chest register
Modulation	Transition from one key to another
Monitor	A speaker placed to enable the performers to hear themselves.

157

Mono	Audio reproduction in a single channel.
Musical Director	Leader of the band
Mute	To stop sound
Nasal	Sound produced through the nose
Non-leaky	Where the vocal folds adduct so tightly in the closing phase that no noise is produced by leaking air
On cue	Agreement to perform a piece of music on a given signal
Onset	The start of a note
Open chord	Chord played on the guitar where not all the strings are fretted
Ostinato	Repetitive rhythmic or melodic riff.
Outro	The last part of a song. The opposite of intro.
Overnighter	An overnight trip between concert locations.
PA	Public Address system. The sound system that delivers the sound to the audience at a concert.
Panning	The distribution of audio between the left and right speakers
Partial	A sinusoidal tone that is part of a spectrum
Patch bay	Device with multiple inputs and outputs for connecting equipment.
Pedagogics	The principles and methods of instruction
Percussive	Consonant-like phonation used in much the same way as percussion instruments
Perfect pitch	The ability to correctly identify notes without the help of an instrument
Pharynx	The throat
Phonation	Production of voiced sounds

Notfabriken

Pitch	The intonation of a tone
Placement	A subjective term used to describe where a tone resonates
Plugging	Publicizing something by mentioning it on TV or the radio.
Podium	A small additional stage used for things like drum kits.
Powerchord	Distorted fifth chord played on a guitar
Preamp	A unit that amplifies a sound signal before being sent on for further amplification.
Pre-chorus	A two or four line section immediately preceding the chorus. Also known as a "Climb"
Pre-production	Preparation phase prior to touring or recording
Presets	Sound and effect settings that have been set or programmed into equipment prior to a performance.
Pressed phonation	Forced phonation with exaggerated adduction.
Progression	The chord series in a piece of music
Promotion	Advertising and marketing
Quantizing	Electronically modifying the timing and duration of notes played by a musician to even out imperfections.
Rack	A box or frame for holding multiple electronic units of standard dimensions
Range	The span of a voice or instrument from the lowest to the highest notes.
Recording studio	Premises with the equipment and acoustic properties necessary to record music
Reflux	Where the oesophageal sphincter fails to close properly allowing stomach acid to back up into the oesophagus and larynx
Register	The range of the voice while maintaining a particular tone quality
Register break	Audible register shift

159

Relative pitch	The ability to correctly identify notes after hearing a reference note
Resonance	Intensification of a sound due to sympathetic vibration
Reverb	Sound effect that creates a continuous wash of echo
Rider	List of artists requirements (catering, décor, entertainment etc) at a performance venue
Rig	Collective term for equipment
Ritardando	Gradually slowing in tempo
Roadie	Person who loads, unloads and sets up equipment and runs errands for an artist on tour.
Root note	Also known as Fundamental note. Corresponds to perceived pitch
Royalty	Payment to writer based on a percentage of the proceeds of the sales of his work or performance.
Sampling	Sound bite transferred to a keyboard for later use
Scale	A series of notes ordered by pitch and according to a specific scheme
Scat	Vocalist's improvised singing of nonsense syllables approximating an instrumental solo.
Sequencer	A recording device found in computers and keyboards.
Side fills	Extra monitors placed side stage to enable performers to hear themselves during a performance
Singer's formant	Spectrum envelope peak at around 2 -3.5 kHz in male opera singers
Sinus	Air filled cavity in a dense portion of the skull bone.
Sinus piriformis	Two pear-shaped cavities at the bottom of the throat that surround the larynx tube.
Sinusoidal tone	A tone without overtones

Notfabriken

Soprano	Female voice classification in classical singing characterised by high pitched singing around c1 to c2.
Sound	The particular qualities of a singer's voice, determined by the vocal folds and the vocal tract
Sound check	Checking sound prior to a concert, rehearsal or other musical activity.
Staccato	Short, separated notes. Opposite of legato.
Stage dive	Diving from the stage into the audience.
Stage left	To the right of the stage when viewed from the audience.
Stage right	To the left of the stage when viewed from the audience
Stereo	Audio reproduction from two separate channels. Can create a sense of depth, breadth, direction and distance.
Strings	Collective name for stringed instruments such a violin, cello.
Support	Controlled breathing and adduction appropriate to the desired note.
Subglottal pressure	The air pressure in the airways below the glottis.
Supraglottal	The area immediately above the vocal folds
Sustain	The period of time a note can be heard after its attack.
Tablature	Simplified notation often used for instruments such as guitar.
Tenor	Classical voice classification with a range of approximately c to c2.
Tessitura	The most comfortable sonically pleasant part of a singers range. Your vocal "sweet spot".
Thyroarytenoid muscles	Muscles running between the Thyroid and Arytenoid cartilages
Thyroid cartilage	The vocal fold is attached to the medial anterior surface of this shield-shaped cartilage.

Notfabriken

Timbre	Sound quality or colour
Tracheal pull	The downward force exerted by the trachea on the larynx. Strongest after inhalation diminishing over the course of the phonated phrase.
Transpose	To transfer a piece of music from one key to another.
Tremolo	Rapid repetition of a note (sometimes perceived as vibrato)
Trill	Rapidly and repeatedly alternating between two adjacent notes
Treble clef	The G clef falling on the second line of the musical notation staff. Used for notating music in the middle and high registers.
Tuning fork	Fork-like instrument that vibrates at an exact frequency, usually 440Hz (note a^1)
Unplugged	Performing without electronic amplification
Vestibular fold phonation	Intermittent phonation where the vestibular folds vibrate eg. distortion and growling
Vibrato	Rapid, repetitive variation in pitch
Vital capacity	The greatest volume of air one can exhale after taking the deepest breath possible
Vocal riffing	More or less improvised vocal embellishments
Vocal tract	Throat, oral and nasal cavities. From the vocal folds to the lips.
Vocalis	The middle part of the vocal fold muscle
Voice	The sound produced by pulsating airflow through the glottis causing the vocal folds to vibrate
Voicing	The way the notes of a chord are arranged
Vowel sound	The sound colour (formant frequency) that allows us to discern between vowels

Waveform	A waveform graph describes the variation of an audio signal's amplitude over time.
Whispering	A form of speech characterised by stretched vocal folds and an extremely breathy sound

Notfabriken

Quick guide to the Exercises

Notfabriken

165

INNEHÅLL

Notfabriken

Be great! Don't imitate...
Contact Voice Centre

Voice Centre, Stockholm, was founded in 2003 by Daniel Zangger Borch as a result of natural development of his work in the music industry since 1984.

The aim and vision of **Voice Centre** is to be in the forefront of vocal methods, teaching, training and research in the rock, pop and soul genres. The work of Voice Centre is of an artistic style and contains a variation of vocal related activities. The main objectives are to train and equip, offering voice coaching, individual and group sessions, casting, consulting, seminars and master classes within the framework of VOCALS.

The **Voice Centre** team consist of a few handpicked vocal professionals with a broad experience from the music industry.

www.voicecentre.se is the website where you can find articles and reviews, practical help and guidelines about the function of your voice. You can find visuals of the vocal chords in action. You can send you questions to the "vocal doctor" and find answers about how to teach or help you with specific issues of your own voice.

Voice Centre is regularly consulted by the artist elite in Sweden. Including; record companies, production companies and a variety of education programmes around Europe.

Welcome!

Daniel Zangger Borch